Highly Sensitive Empaths

The Complete Survival Guide to Self-Discovery, Protection from Narcissists and Energy Vampires, and Developing the Empath Gift.

J. Vandeweghe

© Copyright 2018 - All rights reserved.

The following book is produced below with the goal of providing information that is as accurate and reliable as possible. Regardless, purchasing this book can be seen as consent to the fact that both the publisher and the author of this book are in no way experts on the topics discussed within and that any recommendations or suggestions that are made herein are for entertainment purposes only. Professionals should be consulted as needed prior to undertaking any of the action endorsed herein.

This declaration is deemed fair and valid by both the American Bar Association and the Committee of Publishers Association and is legally binding throughout the United States.

Furthermore, the transmission, duplication or reproduction of any of the following work including specific information will be considered an illegal act irrespective of if it is done electronically or in print. This extends to creating a secondary or tertiary copy of the work or a recorded copy and is only allowed with express written consent from the Publisher. All additional right reserved.

The information in the following pages is broadly considered to be a truthful and accurate account of facts and as such any inattention, use or misuse of the information in question by the reader will render any resulting actions solely under their purview. There are no scenarios in which the publisher or the original author of this work can be in any fashion deemed liable for any hardship or damages that may befall them after undertaking information described herein.

Additionally, the information in the following pages is intended only for informational purposes and should thus be thought of as universal. As befitting its nature, it is presented without assurance regarding its prolonged validity or interim quality. Trademarks that are mentioned are done without written consent and can in no way be considered an endorsement from the trademark holder.

Table of Contents

FREE AUDIOBOOK 7
Free E-book and Newsletter 8
Introduction 9
Chapter 1: Is This You? 11
    Do You Relate to This? 11
    Empath Checklist 13
    You Are An Empath 17
Chapter 2: What is An Empath? 18
    What is an Empath? 18
    Scientific Explanation 19
    Shamanic Explanation 20
    Life and Spiritual Purpose of Empaths 21
    The Gift of Being an Empath 22
Chapter 3: Empath Archetypes 24
    Emotional Empath 24
    Physical or Medical Empath 25
    Geomantic Empath 26
    Plant Empath 26
    Animal Empath 27
    Claircognizant or Intuitive Empath 28
    The Wounded Healer 28
Chapter 4: Self-Assessment: Are You An Empath? 30
    You Are A Great Listener 30
    You May Struggle to Connect to Standard Religion 31
    You Are Drawn to Spirituality 31

You Struggle to Keep Healthy Boundaries 32
You May Struggle with Addictions 32
You Are Likely Highly Creative 33
You Can "Feel" Others 33
You May Have Suffered from Narcissistic Abuse 34
You May Feel Extremely Close to Plants and Animals 34
You Might Have Experienced Mental or Physical Symptoms 35
You May Experience Psychic Attacks 36
You Are Sensitive to Food 37
You Can Feel Collective Energy 38
You May Sense Bad Things Before They Happen 38
Truth Seekers 39
If You Don't Love It, You Don't Do It 40
You Often Feel Bored or Distracted 41
You Want to Heal Others 41

Chapter 5: Growing Up Empathic 43

Growing Up as An Empath 43
If You Had a Narcissistic Parent 45
Parenting as An Empath 46
Parenting Empathic Children 47

Chapter 6: Empathic Re-Wiring 49

Dealing with Low Self-Esteem 49
Unwiring Every Negative Belief You Picked Up 50
Rewiring with Positive Beliefs and Intentions 52
Positive Reinforcement to the Sub-Conscious Mind 53
    Positive Visualization 53
    Positive Affirmations 53
    Goal Setting 54
    To-do Lists 55
    Appreciation and Gratitude Journals 55

Consuming Positive Self-Development Material 56
  Get Away from the Noise – Live by Yourself 56
  Putting Yourself First 57
  Surrounding Yourself with The Right Energy 58

Chapter 7: Empath Strengths 60
  A Great Power 60
  An Amazing Friend 60
  Ability to Detect Red Flags 61
  Detecting Compulsive Liars 61
  Strong Creative Talents 62
  Excellent Problem Solvers 62
  Great Entrepreneurship Abilities 62
  Strong Relation to Animals and Plants 64

Chapter 8: Empath Weaknesses 65
  Attracting Narcissistic People 65
  Knowing Better but Not Doing Better 66
  Taking on Responsibilities that Aren't Yours 67
  Struggling to Live a "Normal" Life 68
  Difficulty with Routines 69
  Weak Boundaries 69
  Tendency to Have Addictions 70

Chapter 9: Empathic Protection 71
  Recognize Red Flags and Walk Away 71
  Recognize and Protect Yourself from Energy Vampires 72
  Save Yourself from Time Vampires Too 73
  Preserve and Protect Your Energy 74
  Shield Your Aura 75
  Leave Abusive Relationships 75

    Carry Protective Crystals or Amulets 76

Chapter 10: Empathic Self-Care 78

    Re-Charge Often 78

    Exercise Your Creativity 79

    Consider Working for Yourself 79

    Practice Energy Clearing Often 80

    Meditate 80

    Hot Showers 81

    Himalayan Salt Baths 81

    Binaural Beats 81

    Get Energy Healing Done 81

    Clear Your Chakras 82

    Practice A Healthy Social Life 83

    Take Advantage of To Do Lists 84

    Have a Gratitude Journal 85

Chapter 11: Ascending Earth Consciousness 86

Final Words 88

FREE AUDIOBOOK

Feel like listening instead?

Save yourself $14.95 and click the link below to get the Audiobook Edition for FREE

For US:
http://bit.ly/Empath_Free_Audiobook

For UK:
http://bit.ly/Empath_Free_Audiobook_UK

Please note: Must be a new member to Audible

Free E-book and Newsletter

6 WAYS TO THRIVE AS AN EMPATH AND LIVE A GREAT LIFE

Click the link below to sign up to the newsletter and receive your free eBook on 6 Ways to Thrive as an Empath and Live a Great Life. I promise, there's a ton of value in it!

http://bit.ly/Thriving-As-An-Empath

Introduction

Thank you for purchasing *"Highly Sensitive Empaths: The Complete Survival Guide to Self-Discovery, Protection from Narcissists and Energy Vampires, and Developing the Empath Gift."*

By purchasing this book, I am assuming you either: a) know you are an Empath, or b) are curious about whether you are an Empath. Either way, this book is the perfect read for you. This book is designed to give you a stronger understanding on what it means to be an Empath, how it has likely impacted you throughout your life, and how you can protect yourself and care for yourself so that you can nurture and master this incredible gift.

Since there is a chance that you may be reading this book wondering if you are in fact an Empath or not, I wanted to start out by including a basic checklist to help you decide "yes or no." If you determine yes, then you know this book is exactly what you have been looking for.

Here is your basic checklist. Mark off any statement that accurately reflects you. You will find a more in-depth checklist in Chapter 1.

- "I am prone to experiencing bouts of anxiety and depression."
- "Crowded places tend to make me feel overwhelmed."
- "I am passionate about helping other people."
- "As a child, I was sensitive to the emotions of others. Especially figures of authority."
- "I often feel drained after hanging out with certain people for too long."
- "My mood seems to change for no reason."
- "I can often feel what others are feeling as though it is happening to me personally."
- "I tend to be introverted, even though I may like spending time with other people."
- "Solitude is where I feel most connected and clear so that I can enjoy myself."

- "My nerves can be overwhelmed from hearing too many sounds or smell to many smells."
- "I have a hard time falling asleep, sometimes I even procrastinate going to bed."
- "Sometimes I can feel the presence of beings who are not actually there."
- "Bright lights and bad smells can shift my mood and make me deeply uncomfortable."
- "I have a deep love for nature."

These bullet points are to give you a basic understanding of what Empaths can experience. If you are still not 100% sure yet, do not worry, we will be taking a deeper look into the Empath traits in the next chapter. Throughout the pages in this book, you are going to learn about what it means to be an Empath and how you can properly care for yourself as one. This will allow you to reclaim your quality of life and begin to experience things that may have previously been too overwhelming for you.

Know that you are not alone in being an Empath, and being one is a highly treasured gift that allows you to bring great value to the world. As you read more, you will grow to understand what this all means and how you can build your gift to begin having a massive impact on the betterment of society, without draining yourself or giving yourself away in favor of this mission.

Enjoy.

Chapter 1: Is This You?

"The only true happiness lies in knowing who you are."
- ***Laurell K. Hamilton***

For many people, discovering a new label for how you identify and who you are can be both scary and liberating. On one hand, you have a new term for who and what you are. This means that you are now "diagnosed" as a certain type of person. However, it also means that you are now able to discover more about yourself. Having a label for who and what you are opens up the opportunity to learn what that means and how it impacts you in your life. As a result, it can be liberating to know that you are not alone and that there are ways for you to create a powerful and enjoyable life with your new label in tow.

Like all other labels, identifying as an Empath is not entirely by choice. Rather, you either are an Empath, or you aren't one. Then, you can choose whether or not you want to *use* the identity. Of course, you can abandon the identity and deny who you are. Or, you can embody it and embrace the reality that you *are* an Empath, and you can begin using great strategies and tools to thrive in life, rather than to live in fear.

Still, before you embody the new label, you really want to make sure that you completely identify. Knowing for certain is essential as it helps us embody who we are and feel more complete in our identity. So, I want you to take a read through the following story. If you relate to it, then you should check over the "Empath Checklist" after the story. If the story doesn't fully relate to you, that's okay, still read the Empath Checklist and see if you can relate to that. Some Empaths have better protection abilities than others.

Do You Relate to This?
You are parked in front of the post office. It's a day like any other: ordinary, plain, and simple. You have nothing big planned, other than to get this package sitting next to you off to your friend. You look down

at it and place your hand on top of it. It's time to go in, but you're not ready. Inside, you feel silly. *"It's just the post office!"* you try to rationalize and reason with yourself. *"Look, everyone is walking in and out like it's no big deal. Why are you so afraid?"* you continue, trying to give yourself a pep talk so you can get up and get going.

You subconsciously count the people as they walk in and out. On the surface, you know this is a simple task. Inside, you are constantly analyzing. Each time a person walks in, you can see their energy and emotions. You have their story in your mind, even though you are not entirely certain as to how it got there. When they walk out, you breathe a sigh of relief in knowing that there is one less energy in the building. Still, you are analyzing. You pay attention to how they leave, what they seem to be feeling, and the rest of the story falls into place in your mind. *"That guy is clearly upset..."* you think to yourself, noticing someone walking in through the door again. Although he does not seem obviously and outwardly upset, you can sense that there is something in his energy keeping him down. Anxiety crawls in as you think about having to enter the building where he, and many others, are filled up with emotions and energies that are overwhelming. You try one last time to get out of your car, but it feels like you can't. *"Come on, this is just anxiety! You got this, let's go!"* you repeat, over and over. On some level, you know it's not anxiety that is holding you back. It's not *you* holding you back at all. It's *them.* All of them. All of their energies raging through, overwhelming the space and causing you to feel stressed out. You know the moment you go stand in line you are going to be analyzing and processing. Only, this time you will not be shielded by the safety of your car. This time, they will begin to notice you and look at you. When they do, you can't help but catch eye contact. And when that happens, well, then you can read the whole story. The energies that swirl inside of you become too much to bear, especially when so many people seem to be staring directly *into* you. You don't know how they do it. You don't know how you notice it. But you know that when you connect with these people, even when there is zero conversation shared, you connect on an insanely deep level. Every. Single. Time.

So instead, you sit in your car with your hand on the package, giving yourself a pep talk. When you are ready, you will hop out and get the package sent. Then, you will be back in your car. Physically, you may appear fine. Your breath may be normal and steady, your heart rate may be calm and even. But inside *somewhere*, you will feel like you are gasping for air and like your heart is racing a mile per minute. That is because your energy is bared to the world and you can feel it, but you do not yet know how to protect it. You are an Empath in need of the energetic tools required to protect yourself and face the world with the ability to possess and *use* your gift, rather than feeling relentlessly abused by it.

Empath Checklist
If you relate to the above scenario, then there is a good chance that you are an Empath. Many Empaths are diagnosed with anxiety and depressive disorders because of how they experience the world around them. Being an Empath does not mean that you do not actually possess these disorders. Rather, it means that you may now have a reason as to *why*.

In addition to anxiety and stress, there are many other things that you may face if you are an Empath. Check off every one that is a "yes" for you.

	You seem to just "know" things even when no one has told you.
	When you know things, it's far beyond intuition or gut reaction. It is a pure, undeniable knowingness. The more you acknowledge it, the stronger it becomes.
	You are overwhelmed by public places.
	You might have certain public places that have a specific energy to them that you love, so you spend more time in these places. They help you recharge.
	When there are too many people around, something unidentifiable inside of you feels "loud."
	When someone around you feels something, you feel it too.
	If someone describes a feeling (physical or emotional), you immediately begin feeling it in your own body or emotions.

	You seem to know people's stories without ever asking or being told.
	You can tell what other people are thinking about you.
	When you see violence or cruelty you feel physically, emotionally, and mentally unwell.
	You may have stopped watching many TV shows and paying attention to the news and media altogether to prevent these painful feelings.
	You can't stand being around bad/negative energy.
	You may now watch a lot of comedies and innocent romance movies and shows that have no violence or true pain in them because they help you feel good.
	If someone is lying, you know.
	If someone is not telling you something, you know.
	When someone is sick or hurt, you may begin to have the same symptoms, even if you come out completely healthy on medical tests.
	If people are pregnant, you may feel sympathy pains or false pregnancies.
	You may have chronic digestive disorders. (This is caused by emotional overwhelm.)
	You may have chronic back, neck and shoulder problems. (From "carrying the weight of the world.")
	It may feel like you are magnetically attracted to the underdog and are always in the right place at the right time to help them.
	You may feel like it is your duty to look out for the underdog, so you do not necessarily mind the previous "symptom."
	You may look out for the underdogs to the point of being overwhelmed and no longer looking after yourself. This can be from looking out for one far too much or looking out for far too many.
	If someone is pained, you will help them. This is true even if they are not willing to admit their pain and they are toxic. Because you know what they are unwilling to admit, you want to "save" them and sometimes (or often) find yourself in painful or abusive situations.

	It may feel like everyone wants to talk to you about their problems.
	When everyone talks to you about your problems, it may make you feel like you have many even if you do not.
	You may feel chronically tired. Sleep may not feel like it provides you with enough proper rest, so you feel like you are constantly too tired.
	You may have an addictive personality, finding yourself drawn to binging on drugs, alcohol, sex, food, or anything else that allows you to feel good, even if only temporarily.
	Metaphysical things may seem fascinating to you: especially healing and holistic therapies.
	When you learn about metaphysical theories and practices, you likely find yourself unphased. Empaths rarely get shocked, even when these things seem "out there."
	You may be extremely creative. It is likely that your creativity is an outlet for you, even if you don't use it as often as you feel you should.
	You feel magnetically drawn to the outdoors, nature, and animals. These are essential in your life.
	You may feel like so much bad happens around you and in your life that it is hard to believe and appreciate the good things in your life.
	It feels like you need to be alone regularly, or all the time, otherwise it feels like life is "too much" for you.
	You wonder why other people can have thriving social lives and you can't seem to.
	You may find yourself regularly feeling bored or distracted if you are not being stimulated. If things are not interesting, you seem to just "switch off" and find yourself drawing or daydreaming.
	It may feel impossible to do anything you do not enjoy. This can make living a modern, socially "normal" life feel virtually impossible for you.
	You likely find yourself only interested in hearing the truth, to the point that everything you do is rooted in finding it.

	Adventure likely feels great to you. Being able to have freedom is important to you, so you find yourself traveling and adventuring through life regularly.
	You identify as a "free spirit."
	You cannot stand cluttered or dirty spaces because they make you feel overwhelmed inside.
	You love daydreaming, and you can spend hours doing it. To you, it's a hobby.
	Routine is imprisoning to you: you cannot stand trying to do the same thing over and over, day in and day out.
	You may find yourself overweight even though you do not overeat and you seem to have no medical issues causing it. (This is a subconscious way of protecting yourself from the outside world.)
	You are an incredible listener. You seem to know exactly what people are saying, even if they are struggling to tell you clearly.
	You have an intolerance toward narcissism, though you may find yourself being stuck around narcissists constantly.
	You can tell how the collective is feeling. Each day of the week, month, and holiday all have their own collective "energy," and you can tell how everyone seems to be doing that day on a collective level.
	You do not own any antique items because the energy associated with them is overwhelming. You would prefer to own new, unused items because they feel energetically "clean."
	You can tell how the energy of food is. You may find yourself unwilling to eat meats because the energy does not feel good to you.
	You can also sense the energy of vegetables and other foods. You may find yourself secretly thanking your food for all it does and feeling energetically attached to it.
	To others, you may appear moody, shy, introverted, or unapproachable. These mood swings are generally caused by taking on too much energy from others.

You Are An Empath
If most of these sounded very familiar to you and you checked most of the boxes above then you can be pretty confident that you are an Empath. Being an Empath is both an exciting and somewhat scary thing. On one hand, you now know what you are, and you can take the proper measures to take care of yourself. The energy that once crippled you sent you through rollercoasters of emotions and caused you to feel overwhelmed and "abnormal" can now be managed and handled. You can even use it as your superpower, helping you master what you are here to do, feel fulfilled, and thrive in life.

However, early on when people realize they are Empaths, they tend to feel overwhelmed. Suddenly, all of your regular symptoms may feel heightened. This is because you are now more aware of them and you are paying attention to them more than you ever have before. As a result, you may find that the next few weeks until you begin to really embody and embrace your protective and self-care skills are extra vulnerable and challenging. For that reason, it is a good idea to make sure that you begin practicing these protection and self-care practices as soon as possible and that you really integrate them into your life. The more you practice and use them, the easier it will become to rely on them and have trust in them. Then, they will begin to support you in having a happier and healthier life that is less overwhelming and isolating.

Chapter 2: What is An Empath?

"Empaths are multi-sensory beings who see "beyond the veil" of people's personas and feel other's innermost emotions as their own."
- *Unknown*

Empaths are a form of highly sensitive individuals that are known for being able to energetically experience the energies of other individuals. Rather than simply experiencing the emotion of empathy, Empaths can emotionally, mentally, and physically sense and feel another person's experience. This enables Empaths to be highly sensitive toward other people. This is both a blessing and a curse, depending on how it is used and cared for by the Empath themselves.

What is an Empath?
An Empath is said to be a person who has a paranormal ability to actually "step into" the state of another individual. Empaths are highly sensitive beings who can literally sense and feel the emotions and feelings of other individuals. If an individual is an Empath, they can sense deep emotions beyond what someone else is actively expressing. This means that even if an individual is highly gifted at hiding their emotions or masking them with other emotions, an Empath can sense, feel, and intricately understand the true emotions of that individual. Not only can the Empath sense and feel these emotions, but they can also understand them on a deep level.

Empaths have the capacity to experience complete empathy toward virtually anyone and everyone else. They can sense it towards family, friends, associates, kids, strangers, animals, plants, and even inanimate objects. Some people are known to be more empathetic toward certain things over others. This is often how we end up with things like "animal whisperers" or "plant whisperers." When this happens, that particular person is known to be more empathetic toward that which they can supposedly "whisper" to. What is really happening is not a whisper, but instead a deep inner knowing of what the other's needs are.

If a person is an Empath, they are not restricted by time and space. In fact, they are not really restricted at all. An Empath can sense the emotions and mental state of people who are incredibly far away. Some can even sense the emotions and mental state of individuals who have long since passed. For example, if they were to visit a museum and see the belongings of someone who existed many years ago but whom has since passed away, some Empaths can step directly into the feelings and energies of that person. This enables Empaths to be deeply understanding and to have a highly unique perspective of the world around them.

Empaths are said to be "poets in motion." They see the world in a wonderfully creative and artistic way. They are generally highly artistic, creating art in every way imaginable. Some may master a particular art form, whereas others may prefer to dabble in a little bit of everything. Empaths see the world in a way that most others don't. To them, each day is a new chapter and the book needs to be written in the most poetic way possible.

An Empath can be virtually anyone. They are not known to be isolated to any particular gender, race, culture, or religion. Empaths exist anywhere and everywhere.

Scientific Explanation
From a scientific standpoint, Empaths are thought to have hyper-responsive mirror neurons. Mirror neurons are a group of specialized brain cells that are responsible for helping individuals feel compassion. These cells enable the individual to actually mirror the emotions of other individuals, allowing them to share directly in the other person's experience. Through these mirror neurons, Empaths can feel when other people are feeling things as well. For example, if your spouse is hurt, you may hurt as well. If your dog is elated, you may begin to feel elated as well. If a plant is thirsty, you may begin to feel thirsty as well.

This mirror neuron system allows individuals to experience high levels of empathy toward others, and it is believed that they are highly active in individuals who are considered highly sensitive Empaths.

Electromagnetic fields are generated by both the heart and the brain in individuals. It is believed that these fields are capable of transmitting information about an individual's thoughts and emotions to those around them. Empaths are believed to be highly sensitive to these electromagnetic fields and are capable of picking up on them and recognizing exactly what information is stored within these fields.

Another reason why Empaths are believed to be so sensitive toward other people is through emotional contagion. Emotional contagion was found in research that showed that people generally pick up on the emotions of those around them and then many will experience and express those emotions themselves. This is what causes an entire ward of babies to begin crying after just one baby cries for any particular reason. So, if one baby is upset because they are hungry and begins crying, the rest of the room will likely begin crying simply because they heard someone else crying. Though, later in life, many people learn to block out these feelings or stay focused on their own. Empaths however, can actually feel these emotions and will regularly experience and express them themselves as well, especially if they are unaware that they are being picked up from their environment and not personally created.

Shamanic Explanation
Shamans believe that Empaths are highly gifted healers. Because they have the capacity to sense and feel the emotions, thoughts, and physical experiences of those around them, Empaths are extremely talented at being able to create a deep connection toward others. This allows them to have an accurate understanding of what another person is going through, thus supporting them in creating and facilitating healing that will actually work for the other individual.

Many Shamans believe that Empaths are specifically meant to be healers. They believe that this is not just a gift they have, but a duty they have here on Earth. Shamans believe that being an Empath means your innate calling is as a healer and that you should pursue this life path. Through being an Empath, it is believed that you have the capacity to discover mental and physical illnesses in individuals in a unique and accurate manner, allowing you to facilitate healing that will truly provide healing to the other individual. When trained and refined, the skill of the Empath is extremely precise. They can also move into the energetic and emotional state of the other person without personally taking on the individual energies, allowing them to "step in" and "step out" of the other person's experience with the sole purpose of gathering information from them.

To follow the shamanistic lifepath of an Empathic healer, it is essential that an individual be properly trained. Operating as an energetic healer when you are an Empath can result in you being left wide open to energies that can drain and overwhelm you. It can also result in poor boundaries that leave you susceptible to being energetically attacked by energy vampires, narcissists, and others whom may lack empathy and are known to exploit those who have a plethora of it, such as Empaths.

Life and Spiritual Purpose of Empaths
Many believe that one of the biggest reasons Empaths are here on Earth is to promote and facilitate healing to the general collective. For years, Earth has been overrun by people who lack empathy and who are unable to feel genuine emotions for other people. These individuals are believed to be responsible for corrupting governments, creating a toxic corporate industry, and otherwise leading the human race in a very monotonous, emotionally-void manner that starves humans of their basic needs. It is believed that Empaths are here to protect us and save us from that.

Empaths often choose to pursue paths that align with some degree of healing. They will either focus their efforts on healing one individual at a time, such as with alternative energy healing practices or counseling, or they will focus their efforts on healing large organizations at a time, such as through massive charities or activism. These paths nourish the Empaths need to see the world doing better and to leave it a better place than it was when they arrived.

Although the exact life and spiritual paths of each Empath will vary slightly, the majority are here to heal and reawaken consciousness. They are actively working toward shifting us all toward a better society that supports each individual, promotes and honors emotional wellbeing, and allows us to thrive throughout our lifetimes.

As an Empath, seeing other people suffer and feeling incapable of doing anything about it is treacherous. It can lead to deep suffering for the Empath themselves, resulting in feelings of inner torture and depression. It is through this need to serve that many Empaths may find themselves getting caught up with narcissists, which you will learn more about during your self-assessment in Chapter 4.

The Gift of Being an Empath
If you have done any previous research on being an Empath, you may be fearful that you have been cursed rather than gifted. Many Empaths are presently experiencing a lot of darkness because they are not being properly trained in how to use their gifts. As a result, they are taking on a lot of dark and painful energies from the world around them. In shamanistic terms, they are stepping into other people's experiences, but are not trained in how to step back out. This can be highly overwhelming and painful.

However, the reality is that being an Empath is actually a gift. Once you begin to learn how to master your empathic abilities, you will discover that you have many talents that Earth deeply needs right now. This means you are highly valuable to us here on Earth! You are capable of supporting the collective consciousness in healing, allowing us to rise to a new state of society where we are all nourished, honored, and supported for our experiences here on Earth. Slowly, as a result of all of the Empaths here working toward our betterment, we will begin to witness positive shifts in major areas of our society. The government, corporate, and many other bodies of society who have been known to have a reputation of being greedy, corrupted, and selfish will all begin to shift toward a healthier and more socially conscious style.

Being an Empath means you are not like the rest of the people who are continually abusing and destroying Earth and everyone and everything that lies in their path. It means that you are here to heal and save us from these experiences. It may feel like a massive burden, but understand that it is actually a gift to be proud of. And, since more and more Empaths are incarnating on Earth at this time, you now have access to a great support system that can help you in bringing your missions into completion in reality. You will no longer have to hope and pray for better outcomes because you and the rest of the Empaths that you connect with will all work together to bring a brighter future to Earth and all who inhabit it.

Chapter 3: Empath Archetypes

"I believe Empathy is the most essential quality of civilization."
- *Roger Ebert*

The word "Empath" itself refers to individuals who are highly sensitive toward others. However, there are actually different types of Empaths who exist. These are known as "Empath archetypes." In this chapter, we are going to explore the different archetypes. See if you can identify with any of these to begin exploring what archetype of Empath you may be.

Emotional Empath
One of the most common archetypes of Empaths is the emotional Empath archetype. Emotional Empaths are known to easily pick up on the emotions of those around them, allowing them to feel the effects of the emotions as if they were yours. This can result in you deeply experiencing the emotional body of others, potentially even expressing and feeling these emotions as if they truly were your own emotions.

As an emotional Empath, your most common symptoms will be that you seemingly randomly pick up emotions that make no sense. For example, say you are shopping at the mall, and there is someone in the same store as you that is feeling intense sadness. You may pick up on this and feel an overwhelming need to cry despite not having a strong understanding of or reason for why this is happening.

Another thing emotional Empaths tend to feel symptoms from is their living arrangements. As an emotional Empath, you may find yourself feeling victimized by the people you live with. Family members or housemates who have overwhelming energies or emotions may create distress for you in your own home. For many Empaths, this can make being at home feel unsafe and uncomfortable. For example, if you have a housemate who has a tendency to be angry and unhappy with their life, you may find yourself regularly picking up on their anger. For you this can resonate as anger within yourself, feeling as though you are now angry as well even though you may not entirely understand why. Furthermore, you may find yourself feeling scared because the amount of anger you feel and the power behind it may feel overwhelming. Therefore, whenever that particular housemate comes home, you may find yourself feeling stressed out, scared, and unwilling to participate in household activities. Simple things such as going into the bathroom to shower or going into the kitchen to get water may feel overwhelming. For some, it may even feel like you are constantly trying to hide from that person to avoid feeling their energy. Even though you can feel it from afar anyway, you want to minimize how much you feel by creating some level of distance between you.

For any human, this type of living condition can be overwhelming and stressful. It can create a sense of feeling like you do not belong anywhere and feeling like there is nowhere safe for you to be. Home is a place where you should feel comfortable to hang your hat and find peace and quiet. It should feel like a sanctuary where you can relax and recharge, not a place where you have to be on your toes constantly prepared to deal with any emotional outbreak that may come your way.

When it comes to being an emotional Empath, it is important that you take the time to learn how you can differentiate between your own emotions and the emotions of other people. If you are not actively capable of doing this, you may begin to feel as though your Empathic abilities are burdensome because you are exhausted from being on an emotional roller coaster that almost certainly does not belong to you. Seeking support and enforcing tools that can assist you in recognizing your own emotions versus the emotions of others can be extremely valuable in supporting your ability to master your Empathic abilities.

Physical or Medical Empath
Empaths that are capable of picking up on the physical sensations and symptoms of others and feeling them within their own bodies are known to be physical Empaths. These Empaths may follow the path of becoming a medical Empath because they have an easier time recognizing and diagnosing ailments in individuals due to their ability to feel what their patient is feeling.

As a physical Empath, you will recognize symptoms such as being able to feel sensations of an ailment that someone is describing to you. For example, if your friend complains that they have a headache, you may immediately begin to feel a headache coming on. This is because you are picking up on the sensations that your friend is experiencing. This does not have to be verbalized, however, for your gift to activate. For example, if someone is in your vicinity who has cancer, you may be able to tell and know exactly who it is without ever having been informed of this ailment, simply because you can feel and sense it.

When you are a physical Empath, it is important that you learn to ground and connect to your own sensations to refrain from feeling and holding onto every single ailment that you hear about or connect to. If you are not careful, you may feel as though you are in a chronic state of pain. Many physical Empaths will be diagnosed with chronic pain conditions such as fibromyalgia for this very reason.

Geomantic Empath

If you are a geomantic Empath, this means that you can attune to the energies and emotions in an environment or place. So, certain places may make you overwhelmingly happy even though you may have been feeling completely neutral coming into the place. Alternatively, some may give you an overwhelming feeling of sadness, anger, frustration, uncertainty, fear, or otherwise. These are all symptoms of being tapped into your environment and drawing on emotions and energies from it.

Empaths who are attuned to geomantic energies regularly need to spend time in nature to relieve themselves from the energies they are experiencing. Being in nature can support them in feeling calm and comfortable, allowing them to rest and recharge so that they can go back into the world and feel safe and secure.

Plant Empath

Plant Empaths are exactly what they sound like: individuals who are highly attuned to plant energy. Individuals who are known to be plant Empaths seem to naturally have a green thumb, being able to easily care for any plant effortlessly with minimal support or prior information. Individuals who are plant Empaths can sense what a plant needs or wants, allowing them to find the perfect environment for that plant to grow in, as well as in knowing when to feed and water the plants.

If you are a plant Empath, you may feel like you receive guidance directly from trees and plants. This is typically sensed by hearing or knowing what they are trying to transmit to you within your mind. As a plant Empath, you may find that you pick up information directly pertaining to the plant's needs, as well as wisdom about life in general.

Keeping a lot of contact with plants and trees and spending time in forested nature is a great way to keep your Empathic senses nourished and grounded.

Animal Empath
While virtually every Empath has a strong connection with animals, animal Empaths have an incredibly powerful one. Individuals who are animal Empaths will generally devote their entire lives to animals in one way or another. They may do this by becoming an animal whisperer or behavioral trainer, taking care of animals through volunteering at organizations, or even becoming veterinarians.

Animal Empaths typically spend as much time with animals as possible as this supports them in feeling connected to their purpose in life. They may find the study of the biology or psychology of animals to be fascinating, possibly even pursuing it to support their mission of supporting animals in every way possible. Because of their gifts, animal Empaths are especially capable of talking to animals in a paranormal way, as well as discovering what ailment they may be facing so that they can promote healing within the animal.

Claircognizant or Intuitive Empath

Intuitive Empaths are known to be claircognizant. This means that they intuitively "know" when something is going on. They can easily detect when people are lying to them, they are able to sense the true emotions and intentions of others, and they can draw information from virtually any person, place, or thing. These individuals are talented at "just knowing" when something is up. Many might claim that they have a strong gut sense or sixth sense that supports them in reading their environment to get accurate feedback from it. Most empaths have these abilities to an extent but not to the level of an Intuitive Empath.

If you are an intuitive Empath, you will also need to make sure that you learn how to step back out of experiences after you have stepped in. You may find yourself stepping into other people's experiences accidentally or naturally, particularly if you are not trained. Knowing how to step back out will allow you to "turn off" the inner voice from time to time so that you can ground and enjoy your reality in addition to being able to use your Empathic gifts as needed.

The Wounded Healer

The wounded healer is a secondary archetype. This means that you can be any other one of the archetypes (or even multiple) and then have this archetype as well. Unlike the others, however, this archetype can be healed. In fact, if you recognize that you have it, it should be healed.

Wounded healers are individuals whom are believed to have suffered a great deal of misery and trauma for their Empathic gifts in past lives. They may have also suffered within this life time too. As a result, they have grown to see their gift as a curse and may feel drawn to attempt to sabotage it or hide it to refrain from being further hurt. This actually hurts the Empath even more, resulting in them not feeling empowered to pursue their life and spiritual missions. Some common symptoms of a wounded healer include: hiding their gift, viewing their gift as a curse, undervaluing themselves when sharing their gift, sharing their gift with the wrong people, or otherwise allowing their gift to essentially curse them.

Healing the wounded healer archetype comes from spending time understanding what caused this secondary archetype to arise in the first place. Then, once you have, you can begin to heal accordingly. If this is from vows you have taken in past lives, you can work together with a past life regression healer who can support you in breaking these vows and empowering your current life. If these are from undervaluing yourself due to being disempowered during your current life, you may want to work together with another healer who does not presently suffer from the wounded healer archetype that can support you in feeling more empowered within your gifts again.

The wounded healer is extremely common and there is no shame in realizing that you may suffer from this secondary archetype. If you do, be sure to seek support in releasing it and know that you are not always going to feel this poorly or wounded around your gifts. You *can* feel empowered once more. There will also be more information on overcoming this later in the book.

Chapter 4: Self-Assessment: Are You An Empath?

"Your sensitivity is one of your greatest superpowers."
- *Unknown*

Now that you have begun to understand more about what an Empath is and the various types of Empaths, it is time to determine whether or not you are one. If you are reading this book and feeling connected to it already, there is a good chance that the answer is "YES!" However, let's take a deeper exploration to see how Empath-like you truly are. The following list is filled with phenomena that Empaths regularly experience. If you feel that you connect to many, most, or all of these phenomena, then there is a good chance that your Empathic gift is extremely strong. In other words, you are extremely gifted!

You Are A Great Listener
Empaths are known to be incredible listeners. In fact, many tend to be the "counselor" in their friend group. You may notice that your friends, family, loved ones, and maybe even complete strangers come to you with their problems and want to talk. At times, it may even feel like you are an emotional dumping ground for people's thoughts and emotions.

As an Empath, you have a strong ability to listen to others and truly feel what they are sharing with you. They especially like talking to you because people feel like you hear what they *aren't* saying and know the problem better than they do, which can be a great relief for many. Modern society is not overly accepting of many thoughts, feelings, or emotions. As a result, many people are uncomfortable or seemingly incapable of sharing these things. Because you seem to "just know," people may be drawn to you because it feels like a breath of fresh air being understood in ways that no one has likely ever understood them before.

You May Struggle to Connect to Standard Religion
Many Empaths find it extremely challenging to connect to the teachings of the majority of modern religions. Although most Empaths will see and appreciate the underlying messages of connection and unconditional love, they tend to pick up on the reality that most religious organizations do not actually live or operate in alignment with these teachings. This can lead to a deep inner sense of struggle for any Empaths who have been raised in or around a religious community. They *want* to see the good in it all and connect with their loved ones, but many see right through the teachings and find themselves feeling frustrated with the deception that seems to go on with many religious groups. Furthermore, Empaths highly value freedom and free will, both of which are rarely honored in religious teachings. For this reason, most Empaths will find themselves being heavily drawn away from religious teachings, perhaps even growing a deep sense of resentment toward them and all that they stand for.

You Are Drawn to Spirituality
Despite not being attracted to religious teachings, many Empaths will be attracted to spirituality. Spirituality tends to be more accepting of and understanding toward Empaths, allowing them to feel understood and recognized by others. This also allows them to facilitate deep connections toward the teachings and the others who follow similar paths. This type of connection can be heavily empowering for Empaths, allowing them to feel supported in their journey as they also support others. Since the spiritual path is filled with Empaths, many Empaths trust that the individuals in these journeys will think similarly to them and therefore will be more accepting, understanding, empathetic, compassionate, and caring towards them. This allows them to feel reciprocated, making it far more inviting than many standard religious teachings.

In addition to supporting them in feeling understood, many spirituality-based teachings actually elaborate on the meaning of being an Empath and support Empaths in understanding themselves and refining their talents. This means that through these teachings the Empath can further their own sense of self-understanding and work more passionately alongside their life and spiritual purposes with clear direction, guidance, and support.

You Struggle to Keep Healthy Boundaries
One symptom many Empaths face is struggling to keep healthy boundaries. Because an Empath can sense exactly what another person is feeling or experiencing, they may find themselves regularly making excuses for the other person. Things such as "oh, they didn't mean to" or "they only did this because deep down they are hurting" regularly come to mind. Although having these deep understandings of others can be valuable, they can also result in the Empath being taken advantage of and used by others with less empathy, or none at all.

The difficulty of maintaining healthy boundaries, or any boundaries at all, for Empaths, can be a major point of trauma. Because the Empath strives to see the good in others, they may let people repeatedly take advantage of them or abuse them because they struggle to connect to the reality that you cannot help someone who does not want to help themselves. You may feel like you have to be the "savior," even though the chances of this panning out are extremely slim.

You May Struggle with Addictions
Empaths are known to struggle with addictions. Many use addictions as a coping method to attempt to "shut off" their empathy or numb them toward the world around them. While this may seem to work, the reality is that nothing can actually shut off their gift. Instead, what often ends up happening is that they begin to dissociate from their feelings and ignore the reality of their empathic abilities. Over time, this leads to a deep sense of depression because they take on an excessive amount of energy and emotion, create even more within themselves, and never effectively deal with or release any of these energies or emotions.

Addictions within Empaths are not restricted to substance abuse. They may also be drawn to overeating, oversleeping or never sleeping to avoid nightmares and restlessness, video games, or otherwise obsessively attempting to draw their attention away from reality to avoid the pain that they are experiencing and suffering with.

You Are Likely Highly Creative
Individuals who are empathic are almost always highly creative. They perceive the world in an entirely different way and tend to see art where others see virtually nothing. For example, an Empath may look at a blank page and see an entire image come to life, thus drawing them into wanting to create that image and bring it into reality. Empaths have visual gifts unlike any other, allowing them to quite literally think things into existence. An individual who is not empathic would likely see just a page that is blank. Empaths are known to become artists on varying levels. They may create art through words, objects, perception, photography, or virtually anything else. The entire world is a canvas to Empaths, and they just want to create. Creating allows them to express themselves in ways that words and emotions do not always allow for. Additionally, it gives them the opportunity to feel incredible self-worth, empowered and inspired by the world around them.

You Can "Feel" Others
People who are empathic can "feel" others. As you may have picked up on in previous chapters, this is actually one of the primary things that identify an Empath. If you can feel others either emotionally, mentally, or physically, or any combination of these three, there is a good chance that you are an Empath. These symptoms allow you to step into the reality of others and experience what they are experiencing in a way that the average person cannot.

When it comes to Empathy, average people experiencing Empathy can relate what someone else is experiencing to something that they have experienced themselves in the past. However, for an Empath, it is much deeper than that. You do not relate people to your own experiences. Instead, you directly feel theirs. This is what allows Empaths to feel things that they have never personally experienced before. For example, if someone were to tell you that they had a concussion, you may feel the exact symptoms they are experiencing even if you have never had a concussion before.

You May Have Suffered from Narcissistic Abuse
Narcissists are drawn to Empaths because they have the one thing that the narcissist completely lacks: empathy. Empaths, as you know, have a heightened level of empathy that is above average. This makes them more desirable than the average person because they have enough to substitute for the lack of empathy that the narcissist has. Furthermore, Empaths are more likely to forgive and desire to see the good in other people. This means that it is easy for a narcissist to draw Empaths into their abuse cycles and quickly turn their empathic gift into a burden that they long to destroy so that they can step away.

If you have ever suffered from narcissistic abuse, or if you are currently suffering from narcissistic abuse, it may be because you are an Empath. If you feel that you are and would actively like support in helping you safely escape and heal from this abuse, or retrospectively understand what was happening during that time in your life, you may be interested in reading my other book: *"Emotional and Narcissistic Abuse: The Complete Survival Guide to Understanding Narcissism, Escaping the Narcissist in a Toxic Relationship Forever, and Your Road to Recovery."*

You May Feel Extremely Close to Plants and Animals
Empaths, especially plant Empaths and animal Empaths, have a tendency to feel extremely close to plants and animals. Even if you are not a plant or animal Empath, you may still find yourself feeling extremely drawn to them. This is because they tend to have a much purer energy, filled with unconditional love. For many Empaths, plants and animals are a breath of fresh air from the corrupted society that many of us live in.

If you find that you are heavily drawn to plants and animals, and especially if you feel like you can communicate with them in a paranormal way, this may be an indication that you are experiencing your empathic gifts. The unconditional love you feel between each other is simply amazing and blissful. You may even feel that your plants and pets are the only things that can make you feel better when things are not going well. If you feel that you receive wisdom and advice from plants and animals, this is your claircognizant gift arising from your empathic abilities.

You Might Have Experienced Mental or Physical Symptoms
Empaths often experience mental and physical symptoms relating to their gift, in addition to the more commonly talked about emotional symptoms. These are not always directly borrowed from someone else, but may actually be the symptom of feeling so many other people's energies so deeply. Many Empaths may actually experience psychotic attacks or episodes because they feel overwhelmed by the amount of energy around them that they are constantly picking up on. Often, Empaths feel like they are a "sponge" to the world around them, which can result in them picking up and holding on to a lot of different sensations.

Some of the common mental or physical symptoms that you are likely to face are those that are related to experiencing chronic high stress. The body can only carry so many different energies and emotions before it becomes too much for it. Then, it begins to maximize its output of cortisol, the stress hormone, causing for you to begin experiencing emotional, mental, and physical symptoms related to personal stress. This could be anything from physical pain to anxiety and depression, and even chronic thoughts based on suicide or self-harm. It is important to understand that these symptoms are often in relation to your empathic gift. They are generally heightened by both you experiencing other people's stress, as well as the stress from feeling these feelings without properly managing them within yourself. In other words, you are not stepping out so the stress is getting blocked within you.

You May Experience Psychic Attacks

Psychic attacks are a common experience for individuals who are Empathic. Psychic attacks are an attack on Empaths with negative energy. This energy is sent either consciously or unconsciously by another individual or entity with the intention of creating or inflicting harm upon said person. These attacks can be felt by anyone in your life, including family and friends, an acquaintance, or in some cases entities that we cannot see. This harm can be intended to create turmoil in the emotional, spiritual, physical, or mental state of the individual receiving the attack.

If you have ever had a psychic attack, you would recognize it through a multitude of symptoms that you might face. One of these symptoms includes feeling exhausted and then having a deep sleep where you may or may not remember having a nightmare. You may have fears in your dreams of being attacked by someone, typically with quite a large amount of violence. You may also feel extreme and unrealistic fears that feel debilitating. There may be no rational explanation as to why you have this fear or why it is so strong for you, all you know is that you suddenly have it. You may also begin feeling much better following a bath or shower as they support you in protecting your energy and freeing yourself from psychic attack. It may feel like you are not in control over yourself or your thoughts which may lead to increased fear.

Psychic attacks feel a lot like psychotic attacks, causing you to feel like you are no longer lucid and in full control of your own body. Many reports they feel like they are standing next to themselves watching themselves go through the motions. While this may be medically rooted, if you are an Empath there is also a large chance that you are experiencing a psychic attack. These attacks are essentially caused by someone else's energy invading into your personal energy space, causing you to begin feeling unwell and even damaged by their energy.

If you are having or have been exposed to a psychic attack, you need to read *Chapter 9: Empathic Protection* and begin protecting yourself from other people's energies. I would also highly recommend seeing a Shaman. A Shaman will be able to understand what is going on from an energetic point of view and be able to deal with the root cause.

You Are Sensitive to Food
Empaths are known to feel their food in a way that no one else can. Many will become vegetarian or vegan because they feel too much negative energy in meats and animal byproducts. However, this is not always the case. Other people find that they can eat meat just fine as long as it has been ethically sourced. Some also like to bless their meat before eating. How you choose your diet will be highly personal, but you may find that it is chosen based on the feeling and energy of the food more so than anything else.

When you are empathic, you may find that you can literally feel what you need. For example, say your energies are feeling off, you may feel that you need the energy that is within carrots, sweet potatoes, or other foods. This comes from your energetic capacity to read your own energy, read the energy of your food, and discover what it is that you need exactly. You may also feel energetically averted to things that may be causing chaos or destruction within your body. For example, you may be naturally averted to sugars and sweets, especially when you are feeling under the weather because your body knows what energy it does and does not need at any given time.

Other Empaths report feeling emotions from their food. For example, they may feel joy and a surge of love and passion when they look at a plate full of foods that give them positive energy. However, they may feel dreadful and even nauseous when they look at a plate of food that seems to radiate negative energy. Being able to feel the energy in their food means Empaths can intuitively eat in a way that nourishes their body well.

You Can Feel Collective Energy
Collective energy is something that typically only Empaths can feel. Empaths will recognize collective energy based on any number of things. For example, if a large-scale tragedy happens such as natural disasters, Empaths can sense and feel the energy of the collective during that time. There may be a large, unavoidable "void" or sense of loss and longing that arises in the Empath. Alternatively, if it is Friday, they may feel a sense of joy and excitement because the collective collectively look forward to the weekend and so the energy of that day is higher. This will be true for the Empath even if Friday is not the last day of work before the weekend for them. For example, stay at home parents or parents who work through the weekend will still feel this excitement if they are Empathic.

Many things can influence collective energy, and Empaths can tune in and sense and feel those things. Their ability to recognize how the general population will be on an energetic level gives them the capacity to read and understand their environment on any given day. This is how the Empath is able to understand the needs of those around them and how they can expect to look forward to the day.

Unfortunately, this can also lead to a deep sense of emotional turmoil for the Empath. For example, if an Empath is tuned into unwanted or uncomfortable energies, they may begin to feel excessively moody even if they are not being directly impacted by anything that is impacting the collective consciousness.

This is actually why many Empaths are finding themselves overwhelmed, stressed, and even traumatized in the modern world. With so much war, fighting, tragedy, and hate crimes swirling around everywhere, many Empaths feel overwhelmed and overburdened by their gifts. You can learn more about this in *Chapter 11: Ascending Earth Consciousness*.

You May Sense Bad Things Before They Happen
Because an Empath can sense and read the energy of individuals and collective, many find that they can actually detect when something bad is about to happen. They may have an unknowing sense of something

being wrong, thus creating a sense of discomfort and distress within the Empath. When this happens, the Empath may begin to feel physically, mentally, and emotionally unwell. Often, restlessness will arise as they wait for the "other shoe to drop."

In some cases, the Empath may be able to intuitively sense where the bad news or tragedy is coming from. However, in most cases, the Empath will simply know that something bad is going to happen. This can be extremely troubling as they are unsure as to what to expect or what to look for. Instead, they simply know that something bad will happen. This can be troubling for anyone, but especially for an Empath who can literally feel the trouble rising.

For the majority of times, the Empath's sense that something bad is going to happen is confirmed. It may be by something fairly small, such as their bank card not working when they are at the gas station, or for something large such as a fatality or a traumatic event. Either way, it is very seldom that an Empath will genuinely feel that something is going to happen and then find themselves wrong in their feeling.

Truth Seekers
Empaths strive to know the truth. They want to have a deep sense of inner knowingness. As a result of being able to know things so deeply and purely, they crave to know *everything* on this level, especially things that they are interested in. When they don't, it can be troubling for the Empath. They may find themselves stressed out, searching for the truth and trying to find that sense of understanding. This can manifest in many ways, including anything from soul-searching to a lifelong dedication to education and studying. By consuming as much knowledge as they possibly can, Empaths give themselves the opportunity to discover information and create a sense of understanding within themselves that satisfies their hunger.

When an Empath does not know the complete truth about something they must know and they do not feel that deep sense of understanding, they will go to extreme lengths to find out. Nothing will be able to get in their way and they will keep 'hunting' until they find the information they have been searching for. Where the average person would usually give up after no success, the Empath persists.

Empaths can feel things incredibly deeply. When they don't, they will often feel empty. Truth enables the Empath to feel full. When they feel full, they are able to feel satisfied and go about life in a way that allows them to genuinely thrive. For that reason, virtually every Empath will be on a lifelong path of knowing and finding the truth. These truths may not always be verified by scientific or factual evidence, though. They may instead be verified by that deep knowingness that the Empath has, allowing them to know within themselves that they are right and that they have landed on the truth. *Their* truth.

If You Don't Love It, You Don't Do It
For an Empath, doing anything they do not love or at least agree with can be extremely challenging. If you find yourself struggling to stay committed to the things you don't love, especially when you also don't agree with them, there is a good chance that this is your empathic gift shining through. Empaths need to feel emotionally invested in all that they do. They want to love what they set out to do. For that reason, many will feel unwell or unhappy in their lives until they find what they love and pursue it.

If you find that you are literally unable to do the things you don't love doing, this is also likely caused by being an Empath. For you, it may feel untrue or unaligned to do the things that you do not love doing. The Empath needs to be feel congruent. Inside, you rationalize this by realizing that there is only one guaranteed life that you have here on Earth and you do not want to waste it being miserable and taking on the energy of avoidance, resentment, and unhappiness.

You are not alone in feeling like you cannot do these things. A way to overcome this is to find a way to love it or make it fun or to find a way to outsource the task. The best option though is to choose a different life path that allows you to have more joy and excitement, and less frustration and depression in your life.

You Often Feel Bored or Distracted
This ties in with the previous trait. Empaths have a deep need to be stimulated. Feeling deeply is almost addicting, allowing them to have a rush of energy and emotion in a way that can only be understood by other Empaths. If you find yourself regularly feeling unfulfilled and thus becoming bored or distracted easily, it may be because you are empathic. In fact, many Empaths are even diagnosed with ADD, ADHD, and other attention disorders. This is caused by their need to *feel*.

If you are often bored or distracted, you need to find things to do that cause you to feel deeply. Many Empaths find great success in reading, watching movies, creating, playing sports, and engaging in relationships that offer great emotional depth. Having access to that capacity to feel, at least most of the time, can help you stay focused when you need to. Whenever you can, make sure that even ordinary everyday tasks have been optimized for feeling. For example, if you need to vacuum, choose a vacuum that brings you great joy or finds a way to make it a game that allows you to feel fulfilled and satisfied. Alternatively, multitask with something that fills you up, such as listening to music or audiobooks. Having at least one aspect of mundane tasks infused with things that help you feel will make it easier for you to stay committed.

You Want to Heal Others
Empaths have a magnetic feeling toward their need to heal others. Many believe that Empaths came here as healers which is why they have this feeling. Because Empaths can feel how deeply humanity and society have been traumatized and "broken," they feel a deep longing and urge to heal this damage. This, according to many, is the true purpose of the Empath. To sense where society is broken and repair the damage so that we can be restored to a society of love and joy.

If you find yourself being called to heal others, this may be as a result of your Empathic calling. Pursuing skills that will support you in healing others, such as alternative medicine, energy healing, counselling, or otherwise, will help you put this healing call to work. Then, you can begin feeling fulfilled by doing work that genuinely calls to your heart and makes you feel as though you are doing what you came here to do. For an Empath, that feeling is both addicting and necessary. That deep sense of fulfilling reminds Empaths why they are here and that their gifts are truly gifts and not burdens.

Chapter 5: Growing Up Empathic

"It's not our job to toughen our children up to face a cruel and heartless world. It's our job to raise children who will make this world a little less cruel and heartless."
- **L.R. Knost**

If you are an Empath, you have been one since birth. For that reason, growing up as an Empath could have been challenging for you. Many Empaths are not adequately supported throughout their childhood, resulting in them feeling disempowered and believing that something is wrong with them. Some will even push to their doctors to test them to ensure that they are not suffering from some form of emotional or personality disorder.

Growing Up as An Empath
Many who grow up as an Empath feel that there is something different about them that other people do not tend to experience. They often grow up feeling overly sensitive and like their emotional symptoms are not well-understood by others in society. Because society is not well-designed for Empaths, it can result in them feeling as though there are not enough resources available for Empathic children to understand themselves and their intense feelings. This generally leads to two things: bullying, and rejecting themselves.

Being unable to know how to emotionally convey yourself in a way that is considered "normal" to society can result in feeling like you are fundamentally wrong. Empathic children often find themselves struggling with low self-esteem issues, low confidence, and difficulty in socializing with others. This is especially present in socializing with the opposite sex. They may find themselves attempting to have a normal childhood but regularly becoming outcast or shunned for their extra sensitives. This can result in them feeling as though they are incapable of fitting in because they do not communicate and share in the same way that the other children do. That is where the bullying and traumatic events can begin to arise for children.

When Empaths are not taught how to handle their energies and symptoms, they can appear to be oversensitive and weak to others. Children in their schools who are not empathic themselves may pick up on these sensitivities and begin to exploit them. This can result in bullying, sometimes in severe cases. As a child, you may have found yourself a victim of bullying that has had lasting, severe consequences for your mental health. Because there are very few resources available to the empathic child, there is not a lot available for them to learn how to manage their emotions and energies and protect themselves against bullying and the many additional energetic challenges that it presents. If you had this experience in your childhood, you might have felt as though you had a lot of care for the others in your school but that no one reciprocated this care. This can lead to feeling like something is fundamentally wrong with you, and like you are an anomaly that will never be loved or appreciated by others. It also means that you will need to go on and rewire these parts of your brain in adulthood to eliminate the traumatic impact the bullying had on you and give yourself the chance to (finally) be free from the bullying. Many empathic children go on to devalue themselves and develop the wounded healer archetype through childhood traumas such as this.

The other side of not having adequate resources to support and educate empathic children is that there are very few ways for these children to develop a complete understanding of themselves. As a result, many will reject the empathic self and attempt to assimilate into "normal" childhood activities. They may begin acting the part of the bully or otherwise behaving in a way that deeply rejects their overly caring side so that they can fit in. This leads to many challenges for the child, including deep feelings of self-rejection and all of the challenges that this type of experience brings along with it.

Feeling unaccounted for, unrecognized, and abnormal in your childhood as an Empath is completely normal. Although it is not a nice or desirable experience, it does happen for the vast majority of empathic children. This is not because there is anything fundamentally wrong with them, but rather because they are simply not understood enough and therefore they are not given the depth of support required to help them feel understood and "normal" as they are.

If you grew up with a classic empathic childhood, you might find that you are now struggling with symptoms of depression, anxiety, and other trauma-related symptoms. These symptoms are completely natural results when you are raised in this way. The reality is, in many cases, there was no way of preventing these things from happening because society can be rough on a child that is extra sensitive. Without access to the right information and knowledge, there was likely no way for you or others in your life to provide you with the support that you needed to successfully grow up empathic without coming out with some degree of emotional repercussions.

The goal now is to learn how to unwire these repercussions from your mind so that you can rewire it in a way that honors and nurtures your sensitivity, rather than making it feel like a. In other words, the tools that you failed to receive in childhood can now be learned and implemented in adulthood to support you in leading a better life where you can truly begin to thrive.

If You Had a Narcissistic Parent
Another side of the coin that is extremely common in Empath children's childhoods is being raised by a narcissistic parent. An overwhelming number of Empaths claim that they were raised in a narcissistic household that lead to a great deal of damage in their lives. Because Empaths are naturally susceptible to the psychological abuse inflicted by narcissists, being raised in a narcissistic household can further damage the child. Since the abuse starts right from a young age, these Empaths are conditioned to use their gift only for the benefit of serving narcissists. They are never granted the ability to see how this gift is powerful and what they can do with it. Instead, they are

conditioned to accept the abuse from a young age and often will go on to find themselves being abused by more narcissists later in life. I discuss this topic far more in-depth regarding romantic relationships in my book *"Emotional and Narcissistic Abuse: The Complete Survival Guide to Understanding Narcissism, Escaping the Narcissist in a Toxic Relationship Forever, and Your Road to Recovery,"* detailing how the victims of these relationships are, in many cases, conditioned from childhood abuse to go on to accept this abuse later in life.

Narcissistic parents can do a lot of damage to empathic children. If you were raised by a narcissist, you may have many of the more damaging qualities of your Empathic gift amplified. For that reason, you may often feel like you are cursed rather than gifted. For empathic children raised by narcissistic parents, it is not unusual to have virtually zero boundaries, an excessive need to please others, and an inability to put yourself first. These are already things that Empaths struggle with, and they are amplified through the trauma and abuse incurred through narcissistic-to-victim relationships. If you have experienced this type of trauma in your childhood and have not yet sought support, you may consider doing so now. Doing so will support you in unraveling the abuse symptoms, as well as in working toward empowering you to feel more confident and strong in your gift of being an Empath. With the right support and healing, you can begin using your empathic gift for good, instead of feeling bound to your abuser through it.

Parenting as An Empath
Later in your life, you may choose to have children. If you do, being an Empath and a parent can be somewhat challenging. The connection we have to our children biologically further enhances the Empathic connection that we have toward them. This means that we feel toward them infinitely deeper than we already feel toward others. If you are an Empath and understand how complex this already is, you can imagine how much more intense it can be with children.

As a parent who is also an Empath, it can sometimes be challenging to raise your children. With so much information out there about what is right and what is wrong, it can be easy to quickly feel overwhelmed and like you are making severe mistakes just for the average person. Add in the Empathic tendencies and it can become downright terrifying. Furthermore, you are more likely to give in to your children and teach them things such as having weak boundaries or taking advantage of other people because you are continually trying to meet their every need. Empathic parents have a tendency to avoid punishing or disciplining children in any way, which means it can be a challenge to teach your child right from wrong.

Other things that may happen if you are an Empathic parent include: having all of the other parents confiding in you, feeling overly protective when your children are experiencing adversity, and projecting your own fears and symptoms unto your children. As an Empath, being a parent can be challenging but also wonderful. You *are* raising the next generation to feel supported and cared for so that they can assist in the ascension of society and Earth. However, you are also among some of the earliest generations at this time to be experiencing life as an Empath to this degree, meaning that you yourself may feel very minimal support and that it can be challenging and frustrating at times in ways that non-Empath parents would simply not understand.

When it comes to Empathic parenting, a good system to look into is using positive discipline as well as attachment parenting styles. When you join these forums and pay attention to blogs that revolve around this topic, you can begin to learn how you can honor your Empathic self while still nurturing healthy boundaries and teaching your children important life lessons.

Parenting Empathic Children

If you are an Empath parenting an Empath, you have a lot of benefits to offer. However, it can also come with its own unique challenges. With two Empaths in the house, particularly if one is younger and the other is still learning about their gifts, some of the challenges you may face include having excessive energies in the home, two overly sensitive beings that may not have the tools to cope, and a tendency to escalate each other's symptoms resulting in two extremely overwhelmed individuals. Being the parent, you know it is your duty to calm things down and lead with a level focus. However, being the Empathic parent, you know this is your duty yet you still may struggle to manage your own energies so that you can be readily available for your child's needs as well.

As a parent who is Empathic and who is raising an Empath child, you are in a unique position to offer your child access to resources (namely, you) that you may not have had growing up. This means that the more you educate yourself on being an Empath and on what it is like growing up, the more support you can provide to your child. While this will not undo all that may have happened to you growing up, it will support you in making sure these things do not happen to your child.

Beyond becoming a resource yourself, it is important to understand that you are still just a parent. You are not intended to be perfect, nor have you ever been expected to be perfect. While you may feel the sting of mistakes deeper than others, realize that you are still entitled to making your mistakes. This is not something that you need to be ashamed of. Own the fact that you are a human and forgive yourself anytime something happens that feels like a "failure." Recognize it as an opportunity to learn and commit to serving and nurturing yourself and your child's needs in a more positive and effective way going forward. Having the support of fellow Empathic mothers and fathers who are also raising Empathic children may be extremely beneficial in this case.

Chapter 6: Empathic Re-Wiring

"Whenever you are on the side of the majority, it is time to pause and reflect."
- *Mark Twain*

If you have been raised in a way that damaged your Empathic abilities and lead to you feeling ashamed about yourself and your gifts, you will likely need to do some Empathic re-wiring. These re-wiring practices will support you in removing the idea that you are damaged or fundamentally "wrong" and will provide you with the ability to regain your position as an empowered Empath. For those who have been raised in abusive or neglectful households that failed to recognize and support your Empathic tendencies, these practices are essential in supporting your ability to heal the wounded healer archetype and regain empowerment and confidence!

Dealing with Low Self-Esteem

As an Empath likely raised by a house that was not understanding of Empaths, your belief system has probably been wired in a way that reduced your self-esteem. Because you were not well-understood growing up, a lot of the beliefs you gained from family, friends, and society itself may have insinuated that you were "broken" and that you needed fixing. In other words, they did not understand you, they were intimidated by your differences, and they wanted to break you down and make you more "normal." This can lead to low self-esteem as a result of not feeling confident in your ability to express yourself as who you are. You may have even learned to express yourself in a way that is not accurate to who you truly are, causing you to feel dissociated from your own identity. If this happened in adolescence when you were in the process of discovering your identity, this could be particularly damaging to your self-esteem.

The best way to regain your self-esteem and increase your confidence levels can be done through a number of ways. The first step is becoming aware of your truth and knowing who you are. If you have made it this far into the book, you have already made step one. If you are just discovering this information for the first time it may take a while to sink in, but once you have developed an understanding of who you are, you can begin to make sense of everything (including your past) and progress to the next steps to improving your self-esteem and becoming a confident Empath. The following practices in this chapter will be extremely beneficial for you.

Unwiring Every Negative Belief You Picked Up

One of the first steps in rewiring yourself is unwiring every negative belief you have picked up throughout your life. This means disassembling your belief systems and replacing them with true, empowering beliefs. This is not an easy task and takes time replacing old beliefs with more empowering beliefs. Once accomplished, it allows you to step into a better reality and live life from your own perspective, as opposed to living a life with clouded judgments influenced by other people's negative beliefs.

To begin the unwiring process, challenge, and question *everything.* Every time you begin behaving as a result of a specific belief you have, question it. Ask yourself where that belief came from and if it truly is yours. If not, begin the process of replacing the old negative belief with your true empowering belief by first identifying the new belief, then reinforcing it by using positive affirmations, visualization, and goal setting. (*See: Using Positive Reinforcement and Motivation.*)

It is important to understand that when you are in the process of unwiring your beliefs to later rewire them with your true beliefs, you must make sure that you are not choosing your beliefs based on popular thinking or opinion. You are your own person, and you are entitled to have your own beliefs, even if they are against popular opinion. Unpopular beliefs are a reality of life and, when they are being honest, virtually everyone will admit that they have a handful of unpopular beliefs. Just because we do not tend to talk about them as often does not mean they still exist. Use your intuition when choosing what beliefs to instill. The beliefs that resonate with you and make you feel aligned to who you are will be the most beneficial.

It is important that you do not endure the entire unwiring and rewiring process only to find yourself coming out the other side with more beliefs that are not true to who you are. This can be a challenge, especially if you are facing low self-esteem and low self-confidence from your conditioning and upbringing, but it is important. Take your time and make sure that as you undergo this process, you also give yourself the space to heal. Healing each layer as you peel it back is an important part of the process. As you heal, you give yourself permission to fully unwire and release all of these negative beliefs and replace them with your own true empowering beliefs, popularity aside.

As you continue to go through this process, you will likely find that there are far more beliefs to be replaced than you initially thought there would be. Since you are an Empath, you have been absorbing beliefs your entire life, whether they were yours or not. As children, we naturally take on the beliefs of our peers and our authorities in society. However, as Empathic children, we take them even further. You may hear one thing one time, and it instantly creates a belief within you, especially if you heard it in childhood. For example, if in the middle of a fight with a parent they told you "you are unlovable." Alternatively, if you hear something repeated to you constantly throughout your life, you can adopt that as a belief as well. For example, in the midst of being bullied, someone may have told you something like "you suck," "you are too fat," "no one likes you," etc. Because of the pain that inflicted, it resonated deep within you and may have become a genuine belief of yours.

Realize that rationality has very little to do with the initial formation of beliefs, especially in childhood. Even if you rationally knew that the belief was wrong or false, you likely still held onto it anyway. This means that as you go along, you will need to honor yourself even when it does not make sense as to why irrational beliefs seem to have such a stronghold in your mind. Instead, give yourself space and recognize that a large part of this rewiring process is healing the beliefs, no matter where they come from. Let yourself release them so that in their place you can input your true beliefs, thus giving you freedom from the false negative beliefs you have been holding onto and allowing you to live a life aligned with your true positive beliefs that serve you.

Rewiring with Positive Beliefs and Intentions

Positive beliefs and intentions are any beliefs and intentions that genuinely align with your best interest. These positive beliefs and intentions can often be contradicted by uninspiring, negative beliefs you have been fed growing up.

When you are in the process of rewiring, make sure that the beliefs you are rewiring with are positive and genuinely serve your well-being and the well-being of others, as well. You can do this by taking a few moments to consider each new belief that you want to affirm to yourself and implant within you. For example, you may have the belief, "money is bad because it makes people evil" which is not a very empowering or positive belief system. Instead, you may want to reframe your perspective and create a new belief, "I will be wealthy and I choose to be loving in how I use my money."

Now, obviously it is going to take some time to replace the old belief with a more empowering positive belief. To achieve full replacement with the new belief, it needs to be ingrained into your sub-conscious mind. That is how the positive belief will actually have an effect on your life.

In order to ingrain the new empowering, positive belief into your sub-conscious mind, you will need to use the power of *repetition*. This is what the sub-conscious mind responds to. Once something has been repeated enough times, it will become "automatic" or in this case "sub-conscious." Think of it like driving a car. When you first started to learn to drive a car, it was incredibly overwhelming as there were so many things to know all at once. But once you practiced enough times, it eventually became sub-conscious and now when you drive a car, you don't even have to think about all the individual tasks required to drive the car.

There are a few ways we can use *repetition* when it comes to new positive beliefs. We will go through this into greater detail in the next heading, *"Positive Reinforcement to the Sub-Conscious Mind."*

Positive Reinforcement to the Sub-Conscious Mind

There are a few tools we can use for positive reinforcement to the sub-conscious mind. A combination of all these tools used repetitively over time will have astounding effects on instilling your mind with positive, empowering beliefs and thus a much better and happier life. These tools include:

Positive Visualization
You might not have experienced it yet, but Empaths have great potential to be creative. Positive Visualization can be a great way to use that creativity you contain and is also a great tool to support your mind in genuinely being able to see a positive future. It gets your mind working and starts the manifestation process. Imagine the ideal situation you'd like to be in a few years from now. Where is that place for you? What does it sound like? Who are the people around you? What do you look like? How do you feel? What luxuries are there? For many, visualizing positive things happening for them is a challenge. If you can begin to practice incorporating positive visualization into your daily life, it becomes easier and easier for you to see, believe and work towards what you desire to have. Then, it becomes easier for you to actually have it. Pick a time of the day that best suits you to do some positive visualization.

Positive Affirmations
Positive Affirmations are a great tool to add to visualization because they support you in having a positive, can-do attitude toward achieving your goals. It can be very powerful to start writing, reciting and listening to positive affirmations of things you would like to be or have in your life. When repeated on a daily basis, it will start to mold your mind and perspective towards positivity. Examples of some

empowering positive affirmations include:

- I have the power to create change
- I forgive myself for my past
- I am worthy of love and joy
- I am worthy of a fantastic life
- I am a creative being
- Positivity is a choice I choose to make everyday
- I choose to be happy and completely love myself today
- I am becoming a better version of myself each and everyday
- Beautiful things happen to me
- I do not seek approval from anyone. I am enough
- I only surround myself with positive and encouraging people
- I am deserving of an abundant lifestyle
- I am successful
- I take responsibility for my successes and failures
- I will accept nothing but the best
- New opportunities come easily to me
- Positive energy surrounds me
- I set clear goals and work to complete them everyday

Goal Setting
Goal Setting is incredibly important because it takes your dreams and desires into account and gives you a real focus toward achieving them and bringing them into your reality. There is something incredibly powerful about writing down your goals. By writing a goal down that you want to achieve in the future allows the goal to become more real in the mind. Once the goal has been written down it becomes easier to break the goal down into smaller goals in order to achieve the desired goal. Another benefit of writing down your goals is it allows you to be reminded of the goal every day and remain focused. Something like a whiteboard can be a great addition to your bedroom so you can see your goals every day when you wake up. Add some pictures or photos next to these goals for more motivation. Make it become more real in the mind.

To-do Lists
To-do lists are a great addition to goal setting. When we set out to achieve big goals (that could take months to a year to achieve), what can often occur after a few weeks is we can feel we have not made any or very minimal progress and it can become easy to feel demotivated. To-do lists are a great solution to this. When we desire to achieve a big goal, we need to break that goal down into many smaller steps. Steps that can be done on a daily basis. These steps need to be written down in our To-do list and when we complete each specific task we can cross it off which is going to give us that beautiful feeling of accomplishment and progression. We will start to feel like we are getting closer to our goal one step at a time thus making us feel even more motivated. When we don't have that To-do list it can become easy to forget about all the progress we have made and focus on how much more we still have to go.

A free website I like to use for my To-do list is; www.todoist.com It enables you to add and cross off all your tasks very easily.

Appreciation and Gratitude Journals
The 4 tools I have previously mentioned are all great tools for your mind to focus on a better future. This particular tool, Appreciation and Gratitude Journals are a great tool to pause and reflect on the present moment and recognize all the things you are grateful for. It can become very easy to get caught up in the future which can leave us unsatisfied at times because we are always wanting more. It's important to stop and take the time to appreciate what we have in life.

The powerful thing about taking the time to recognize what you are appreciative for and writing this down in your gratitude journal, is that you actually increase your vibration and you will naturally attract more things in the future to be grateful for. Crazy right?

It can also be an effective method to shift your perspective when you feel like you 'have the world on your shoulders' and things aren't actually that bad. Another way I like to practice my appreciation is when I have a 'little win' or some beneficial event occurs for the day, I will take a moment to stop and give my gratitude to the Universe. You will be surprised how much this tool will benefit your life.

All of these five tools will work best collectively to encourage you, motivate you, give you hope, improve your self-esteem, and inspire you to keep pushing in a positive direction.

Consuming Positive Self-Development Material
Another great way to rewire your brain is to continually consume positive self-development material. Reading and listening to materials that are designed to inform you about new perspectives, share opinions with you, and support you in rewiring your brain to a more positive mindset are all extremely powerful in unwiring your brain from negative conditioning you received growing up.

It will be especially beneficial if you consume content that is specific to Empaths, as they will be more mindful of how you actually experience the world around you. This type of material can serve you by educating your mind and rewiring your subconscious to let go of beliefs that no longer serve you and replace them with beliefs that will empower you, build your self-esteem and self-confidence, and support you in using your Empathic gift for wonderful things.

I personally love audiobooks. They allow me to consume the information much faster and I can multi-task while listening to the audiobook. Whether that be driving in the car, cleaning the house or walking on the treadmill.

Get Away from the Noise – Live by Yourself
When you are seeking to rewire your brain, it is important to give yourself the space to discover who you truly are and learn what you want to learn. One of the best ways of doing this is living on your own

at least for a while. This gives you a chance to be completely alone and experience who you truly are, free of the pressure of anyone else in your life. It is also a great way to rid yourself of any bad, negative energy that you might have been absorbing.

If you are unable to live alone because you already have a family or you are under conditions where you have to live with other people, consider spending a significant amount of time on your own. Schedule regular breaks and times to be completely by yourself. While this won't be exactly the same, it will give you the opportunity to hear yourself think and figure out what you like to do when you are by yourself. This can support you in having a deeper understanding of who you are, and therefore a greater confidence in expressing yourself.

Even if you can travel somewhere for a period of time by yourself, I would highly recommend this. Get away from the noise and hear yourself think. Take the time to reflect.

Putting Yourself First
Empaths are known for struggling to put themselves first, no matter what the situation is. Many will continue to put others first even long after they begin paying the physical, mental, and emotional price for this behavior. This is a significant symptom of the wounded healer.

As Christopher Walken said, "When you naturally have a healing aura, you attract a lot of damaged people, and having them in your life could drain your energy to the max. A reminder that it is not your job to heal everyone you encounter. You can't pour from an empty cup. Take care of yourself first." Putting yourself first is one of the most selfless things you can do. If you truly want to support other people, putting yourself first and taking care of yourself with the highest quality of care and compassion will support you in being mentally, emotionally, and physically available to support yourself and others for a long time. Treasure yourself in every way possible, and always put yourself first. Be willing to say no, and practice setting boundaries so that you do not deplete your own energy in favor of someone else's needs. Stop tolerating bad energy and negative people.

Surrounding Yourself with The Right Energy

As Jim Rohn said, "You are the average of the five people you spend the most time with." Simply put, energy is contagious. If you are spending time around people with negative energy and are regularly reinforcing negative beliefs around you, you are going to feel an integration of negative energy and beliefs in your own life. Even the most experienced Empaths who have been masterfully protecting themselves and their energy for years find themselves adopting the negative energy and beliefs of those they are around, especially on a regular basis. With Empaths, the people we are emotionally close to seem to have the ability to penetrate through our protection. Although we can work harder to create protection that is impenetrable, consistent exposure can lead to "leaks." Think of it like having constant pressure on the other side of your bubble. Eventually, no matter how hard you try, the bubble can and will burst. If you spend too much time around negative energy and negative beliefs, it will affect you no matter what. It is best to focus on surrounding yourself with the right positive energy rather than trying to fight the negative energy.

Spending majority of your time around people who you can share a positive and healthy relationship with is very important. This does not necessarily mean that you need to discard your old friends and those who you hung out with most. Rather, it simply means spending less time with them in favor of spending more time with people who help you feel great. When you spend time with people who have a positive energy and a set of positive beliefs, you begin to foster these in the same way that you would with negative energy and beliefs. This means that you can begin to experience greater joy in your life. For many Empaths, surrounding themselves with the right group of friends can feel like they are finally coming home to the family they always wanted. It can truly be life changing.

If you are unsure as to how to find a tribe of friends who will be this positive influence in your life, turning to the internet tends to be a great way to start. Beginning too many friendships in search of "the right ones" can be challenging and exhausting, especially for Empaths. Giving yourself the opportunity to meet people online first and get to know them more before building a true relationship with them can be a powerful way to get to know new friends. You can also begin spending more time in areas where more spiritual people hangout. Metaphysical and folk festivals tend to be filled with people who are more Empathic, allowing you to have access to a wealth of new people you can begin hanging out with. There, you may just meet the friends that will change your life. This could be something that you could add to your positive affirmations. I also want to note that as you become a better version of yourself over time and increase your vibration, naturally, you will start to attract higher quality people into your life.

Meeting new friends, especially in person, may be a great way for you to begin using your gift as well. Try relaxing your mind and starting from "neutral" when you are making new friends. Then, allow yourself to read their energy using your gift. Consider what knowingness comes through for you. If it is positive and resonates, there is a good chance that the friendship will become a great one. If it is negative or feels misaligned, then you know that you do not need to invest too much time in building that relationship because it likely will not become fulfilling for either of you in the end.

Chapter 7: Empath Strengths

"The opposite of anger is not calmness, it's empathy."
- *Mehmet Oz*

Empaths have a great deal of strengths that support them in living complete, wonderful lives. When you begin to come to terms with your identity as an Empath and you integrate protection and self-care measures into your life, working in alignment with your empathic gift will become easier. This means that you can begin to enjoy the many benefits and strengths of being an Empath.

Here are some of the wonderful strengths you can look forward to developing and embodying when you awaken to your empathic abilities and begin to take control over them:

A Great Power
Empaths are extremely powerful. This is one of the reasons society puts them down so much. They are afraid of their power. As an individual who can sense things about people that they may not be willing to share, or who can deeply connect to plants and animals around them, you possess clear differences from the average person. In modern society, there are a lot of individuals who are deeply disconnected from the world around them. They struggle to tune in on basic levels, never mind as deeply as you do. You may see it as a weakness, but that is only because you have been conditioned to. In reality, you possess a great power. Once you learn to embrace it and use it to your advantage, you will be unstoppable in creating positive change in the world.

An Amazing Friend
Anyone who has an Empath as a friend should be incredibly grateful. Empaths are amazing friends. Empaths truly cherish the people they love in their life and will go to extreme lengths to help and protect them. They give great advice to their friends. When a friend has a problem or some sort of difficulty, Empaths are happy to use their

beautiful gift of empathizing and putting themselves in their friend's shoes to understand the particular situation and figure out what the best possible decision is.

Ability to Detect Red Flags

Because of your ability to see what is going on beneath the surface, you have an uncanny ability to detect red flags in any person or situation. You do this by empathizing with the other person, essentially allowing you to step into their shoes. This means that you can detect the harmony between the person's words, actions and feelings. There, you can determine whether they are acting in alignment with the truth or if they are lying or being dishonest in any way. By sensing any signs of incongruence, you are able to detect possible ulterior motives.

Whether or not you choose to actually recognize and act on these is a completely different story, but your ability to detect them and become aware of them is extremely powerful. You are capable of knowing any time there is something inherently wrong about a situation, making it easy for you to avoid danger and energetic attacks if you are tuned in and capable of acting on this information. If you are not yet, do not worry. As an Empath, you are capable of tapping into this ability at any time. It is not too late for you.

Detecting Compulsive Liars

Another great ability you have with being able to tell what is truly going on under the surface of others is that you can easily detect compulsive liars. When people are lying, you know it almost instantly. Just like the red flags, you can detect the harmony between the person's words, actions and feelings. By recognizing any signs of disharmony, it can be easy for you to suspect lying. This often comes as just a "knowingness" within. This encourages you to refrain from believing them and can support you in preventing yourself from getting drawn in and trapped in their web of lies. The more you practice this, the better you will become at using this gift.

If you are a wounded healer and not able to utilize your gift efficiently, you may find yourself getting trapped into a person's web of lies. This is something important to address in the process of healing this archetype, if you have it.

Strong Creative Talents
Individuals who are gifted Empaths are known to be very strong in their creative talents. As we have already discussed, they are skilled artists, singers, poets, writers and creators in general. Empaths view the world in a poetic way that enables them to create unique art pieces that highlight their unique view on the world. Their ability to visualize something in their head and bring it into the material world with their creativity is simply amazing. The challenge for most Empaths is first eliminating all the negativity they have absorbed growing up. This negativity could be in the form of doubt, insecurity, fear of failure, and lack of confidence.

Virtually every Empath has the potential to be creative, though how they express or use the trait may vary. In other words, not every Empath will be great at the same thing, but they all will have some degree of creativity that they can use to express themselves and serve the world. This is incredibly satisfying and fulfilling for the Empath.

Excellent Problem Solvers
When an Empath has developed their empathic gift, they can be excellent problem solvers. Using their empathetic ability, they are able to analyze the wants and needs of different parties from multiple points of view. By being able to analyze a certain situation and see many different points of view, gives the Empath a great edge to be able to come up with the best possible solution that will be beneficial for both parties.

Great Entrepreneurship Abilities
Because of their intuitive abilities and their superb ability to solve problems, Empaths make great entrepreneurs. They are highly focused

on delivering the best results to their clients, no matter what their line of work may be. Furthermore, they are heavily driven by a desire to have freedom and to escape from the toxic, overwhelming, and greedy environments of traditional 9 - 5 jobs.

Empath entrepreneurs are great at coming up with creative companies that reach the needs of their clients in ways that larger companies tend to overlook completely. They typically find themselves in their own companies that offer some form of healing or shifting modern society. Counselors, life and business coaches, alternative healers, artists, writers, and other career paths are extremely common for Empaths to choose. Fortunately, each of these can be done on an entrepreneurial basis. They are also excellent choices as they cater to the unique strengths and weaknesses of the Empath, allowing them to shine their brightest and serve in the way that their soul needs to shine.

If you are an Empath and you are not presently on the path of being an entrepreneur, you may find great joy and benefit in beginning this life path. With your gifts and abilities, you have the capacity to begin your life as an entrepreneur and create great success in doing so. There are many great benefits to choosing this career path. Some of these benefits include:

- You are able to experience much more flexibility and freedom in your life compared to working a job
- You can control your own working schedule and holidays
- You do not have to deal with the draining and toxic environments of a 9-5 job
- You can choose the people you want to work with or work solely online
- You can work from home
- You have the potential to earn much more than what a job can offer you
- You can put your creative ability to good use
- Become more fulfilled and happy in what you do
- More travel opportunities may present themselves to you

- General health and happiness will improve when you remove yourself from negative, toxic work environments

Many people believe that empathic entrepreneurship is the way of the future. As more and more people seek to lead a more socially conscious and responsible life, many are avoiding large businesses and corporations that are typically known for being irresponsible, unkind, and savage in their business dealings. These exact same people are seeking entrepreneurs running their own socially responsible businesses in a way that genuinely serves their needs on a personal level. As an Empath, you have exactly what it takes to serve in this way, meaning that you and your gifts are exactly what these people are looking for.

Strong Relation to Animals and Plants
Another great strength possessed by Empaths is their connection to animals and plants. As you know from animal Empaths and plant Empaths, these individuals have incredible talents when it comes to communicating with animals and plants. This is a breath of fresh air in a world where very little concern has been shown to the environment and those who inhabit it. Many humans in the modern world rarely consider other humans, let alone other species or life forms. As an Empath, you may have a powerful ability to relate to these life forms and protect them from the destruction of humans who experience little to no empathy in their lives.

Animals and plants are also believed to be Empathic, meaning that you may find that animals and plants respond well to you, also. You may find yourself attracting animals into your life and having an uncanny ability to help plants thrive in a way that others may struggle to do. This is because they are intuitive and can sense that you are kind. This allows them to automatically trust in you and feel safe, protected and nourished in your presence. They sense your energy, and it supports them in thriving.

Chapter 8: Empath Weaknesses

"We are a slave to our emotions when we don't acknowledge or fear their teachings – be brave through empathy."
- *Christel Broederlow*

As with anything, Empaths also have weaknesses. The weaknesses you face may be debilitating for you, depending on how much you experience them. Unfortunately, most Empaths are not aware of what they are so they end up going through life living in fear of their weaknesses. This prevents them from developing their strengths and can result in them feeling overburdened by their gift. Trust that if you recognize or relate to any of these weaknesses, recognizing them and giving yourself the space to come to terms with them is important. This is where you can begin to heal them and step into your power. As a result, you can keep your weaknesses in check as you give yourself the space required to develop your strengths. Then, a natural balance will arise, and you will have the opportunity to live a life in alignment with your gift.

Attracting Narcissistic People

One unfortunate weakness of Empaths, even stronger ones, is attracting narcissistic people into their lives. Although you might feel intolerant toward narcissists, you may also find yourself overly surrounded by them. The reason why this happens is simple: you have the one thing they lack. Empathy.

Narcissists are drawn to people who have excess empathy because they can exploit that empathy to get what they want. They also love people who have a low sense of self-worth and low self-esteem. If you are not careful, they can exploit you to have their own selfish needs met. This can result in Empaths finding themselves trapped in narcissistic relationships that drain them of their energy and cause them to feel overwhelmed and taken advantage of. Unfortunately, because you can see from the other person's perspective and many narcissists are believed to be narcissistic as a result of childhood trauma, this can result in you siding with the narcissist. Your desire to heal others may result in you attempting to save someone who cannot be saved. That is unless they choose to save themselves.

If you find yourself being surrounded by narcissists or recognize narcissistic relationships presently or previously in your life, this is likely because of the fact that you are Empathic. When not properly protected, you can easily be disillusioned by narcissists who can result in a lot of trauma in your own life. If you *are* presently in a toxic relationship with a narcissist, my book: *"Emotional and Narcissistic Abuse: The Complete Survival Guide to Understanding Narcissism, Escaping the Narcissist in a Toxic Relationship Forever, and Your Road to Recovery,"* may be the answer for you. This book can support you in understanding the nature of the abuse and finding a safe way to free yourself from it in a way that is compassionate and nurturing toward your unique empathic needs.

It is important to understand that even if you are finding yourself surrounded by narcissists, there is a way to protect yourself and you are not doomed to being abused and hurt by narcissists for your entire life. As you strengthen your protection abilities, self-worth, self-care and heal from your mistrust in yourself and your inner voice, you will begin to find it easier for you to identify and recognize a narcissist. Then, you can avoid them in favor of healthier relationships.

Knowing Better but Not Doing Better
Empaths have a tendency to know better but not actually do better. This is not because they don't want to do better, but because they are conditioned to think of themselves as "wrong." Through bullying, societal conditioning, and other abandonment in childhood and young adulthood, Empaths are taught that their inner knowingness is false and that they should not believe it. This causes doubt in the Empaths intuition. If this has happened to you, you might find it difficult to trust and act on your inner knowingness. As a result, you may find yourself missing out on opportunities or kicking yourself for not acting sooner. This is extremely common. Feeling like you should have acted sooner because "you knew better" is a really common feeling for Empaths.

It is important to note that until now, even if you *did* know better, you didn't do better because you genuinely couldn't. Your conditioning resulted in you feeling and believing that you were truly unable to act on what you felt you knew. As a result, you did not act. This is not your fault. If this is something you face, healing your trust in yourself, your intuition and strengthening your sense of self-worth and self-confidence will help you in believing your gut reaction and feeling confident in your inner knowingness. Then, you can begin knowing and doing better. As a result, you will feel like you are living in greater alignment with yourself and you will have fewer instances of feeling like "I shouldn't have done that!" or "I should have done this!"

Taking on Responsibilities that Aren't Yours

As an Empath, you may find yourself taking on responsibilities that are not yours. Empaths have a sense of duty that is hard for them to avoid. Knowing things on a deeper level leads to you feeling like it is your responsibility to do the things that others are not doing. This is because you feel that if you don't, no one will. As a result, you may find yourself struggling to balance too many responsibilities, many of which are not rightfully yours. Many Empaths report feeling like they are "carrying the weight of the world on their shoulders" when they experience these symptoms.

Taking on these responsibilities can manifest on a personal level, a collective level, or both. You may find yourself taking on other people's responsibilities directly in your life. For example, at work, you may realize that people are not doing their complete jobs because of personal struggles. As a result, you take on their responsibilities for them. This can be kind, but it can also lead to you being overwhelmed and taken advantage of. You may also find this happening in other areas of your life as well. Many Empaths take on the responsibilities of others and become taken advantage of, by anyone from friends and family, to coworkers and even parents of other children if you are a parent yourself. It is important to realize that you still need to put yourself first. Helping people is great but you still need to keep a balance in your life and establish healthy boundaries. We will go into more detail about this in the next chapter.

On a collective level, Empaths may take on more responsibility by feeling like it is their duty to heal the world of major tragedies. For example, you may find yourself feeling as though you are personally responsible for healing world hunger, ending war, or finding homes for the homeless. This can result in a constant sense of feeling unfulfilled because no one person can heal these ailments in the world.

Struggling to Live a "Normal" Life
Many Empaths struggle to live a "normal" life. Because of how pain has integrated itself into everyday life and into the conditioning of society, many Empaths find themselves resenting normal life on every level. Still, they may also find themselves longing to live one. This can create inner conflict for any Empath. On one hand, leading a life numb to pain and filled with misery is unbearable. On the other hand, you may find yourself just wanting to fit in. It may feel like you have *never* fit in and you may blame your inability to be "normal" for the reason why you feel as though you never fit in. This can result in you feeling the inner conflict.

As an Empath, going to a mundane job that you dislike filled with people who are plagued by negative energy can be nonsensical and depressing. You may find yourself struggling to assimilate into this standard life. You may even become physically, mentally, and emotionally sick from trying to live this lifestyle. For many, there seems to be no alternative. This is why a growing majority of Empaths are choosing the entrepreneur path. Not only does it provide freedom from these soul-sucking experiences, but it also gives the Empath an opportunity to do something that truly has meaning for them.

The feeling of struggle does not end with career, either. Many Empaths struggle to perform everyday activities such as going shopping, spending extended amount of time with friends or family, or even watching certain things on TV or scrolling through social media. Because of their heightened sensitivities, this can be truly draining and overwhelming for an Empath.

Difficulty with Routines
Empaths and routines are typically not something that mixes well. Empaths tend to find themselves struggling to deal with routines. As you may recall, Empaths feel things deeply and intensely. Often, this leads to an Empath always looking to have some sense of feeling that creates a deep sense of fulfillment.

You may find that you struggle to create routine in your life and that staying aligned with a routine for any length of time is virtually impossible. You crave spontaneity, mystery, and change. In there, you find feelings that you love to explore and enjoy. This results in you feeling fulfilled and alive. For you, routine may create numbness and a lack of emotional fulfillment. Finding ways to be spontaneous is a great way to ensure that you live your best life.

Weak Boundaries
Empaths are known to have weak boundaries, especially early in their development. Your ability to feel people deeply results in you regularly giving people the benefit of the doubt, often stepping into a dangerous cycle of allowing them to take advantage of you over and over again. This can be traumatic for Empaths who do not realize that they cannot save someone who has no desire to help themselves. You may have even been conditioned to abandon your boundaries from a young age, further weakening your boundaries. If this is the case, then you may already be aware of the symptoms you experience in your life as a result of weak boundaries.

Weak boundaries can also occur from a low sense of self-worth and self-esteem which is common in Empaths. When you do not value yourself highly as an individual, you are more likely to tolerate toxic people and toxic environments. Having strong boundaries is all about saying "No!" more often and having no tolerance for anyone treating you wrongfully. Remove yourself from people and environments that do not have a positive impact on your life. As you work to increase your sense of self-worth and self-esteem and respect yourself more, you will naturally develop stronger boundaries.

Tendency to Have Addictions

If you are not adequately supported in your empathic gifts, you may feel drawn toward having addictions to support you in numbing out the pain and "trying to fit in." Many Empaths are reported to have "addictive personalities" because of this. It is important to understand that this behavior in an Empath is often rooted in a desire to relieve themselves of the pain that comes from feeling other's pain so deeply. This can add to the complexity of the addictions, meaning it is important to seek professional assistance in relieving these addictions should you find yourself facing them. Finding professional support that understands Empaths can be extra helpful, although it may be more challenging to find. When trying to remove an addiction, I would recommend replacing the particular addiction with something else in your life that is going to have a positive impact on your life. This could range from training at the gym, playing a team sport, learning how to dance, learning how to play a musical instrument or starting your own business.

Chapter 9: Empathic Protection

"When I peeled back the layers, I found a beautiful resilience inside. This is how I know I will always thrive."
- *Lori Schaffer*

One of the biggest reasons why being an Empath can be considered a "curse" is because many people are not educated in how they can protect themselves from the harsher symptoms, such as carrying too many energies, stepping into someone's experience without being able to step back out, or not knowing how to refrain from stepping in overall. Knowing how to protect yourself can have a powerful impact on empowering you to elevate from the wounded healer to the empowered Empath. Here is what you need to do.

Recognize Red Flags and Walk Away

One of the gifts of being an Empath is that you can quickly detect red flags in situations or people. It is easy for you to identify compulsive behaviors such as lying, exploiting others, or otherwise being abusive or negative toward those around you. Being an Empath means that you can identify these and can then walk away. For some Empaths, the walking away part is particularly challenging. If this is you, learning to walk away is important.

Walking away from situations that do not serve you is not selfish. Many Empaths mistakenly believe that they need to "save" other people. This leads to them getting caught in situations where they perpetually feel responsible for someone else, despite this not being true. Your gifts were not given to you so that you could live in a world of abuse and experience direct damage as a result. They were given to you so that you can save the world. That is likely why you get caught up in your desire to save individual people: it is your nature to "save." However, many Empaths are not taught to understand what this actually means.

You come here to save the planet from a lack of empathy and compassion, but not with the personal responsibility to take on the energy of every individual you meet. Instead, you can help by empowering, uplifting, and inspiring other people to do better in their lives. Those who desire to do better will follow your example and find themselves being saved *by themselves*. You are not here to save them: you are here to show them how to save themselves. This means that your only responsibility is to save *yourself* and lead by example. Through this, you will inspire others to do the same.

Recognize and Protect Yourself from Energy Vampires
Energy vampires are people who can drain a great deal of energy from you. They tend to have problem after problem, and they constantly come to you, asking for more than a reasonable amount of support. As an Empath, you feel into their position, empathize with them, and find yourself feeling personally responsible for providing them with the energy required to do what is needed from you. This quickly turns into a treadmill, where you are constantly running to meet the energy needs of the person but you are never able to fulfill their needs. This is because they are an energy vampire.

In order to protect yourself from energy vampires, you need to teach yourself how to say "no." Learning to say no and stand behind it is important. This is how you can support yourself in feeling confident and protected in saying no. When you say no to an energy vampire, make sure that you consciously say no with your energy as well. Some people will envision their protective shield blocking out the request, preventing the energy from coming into their space altogether. Keeping out the energy of the energy vampire is important. If you let it in, it can begin to create empathic sensations within you that might cause you to change your mind. This is less of a worry when you become stronger in protecting yourself, but early on you are susceptible to changing your mind as a result of this energy.

Recognizing energy vampires and learning how to say no to them will also require you to protect yourself from shouldering any further responsibility. Affirming to yourself that it is not your duty to fulfill other people's needs beyond what you feel is reasonable is important. If you are not doing it out of love for yourself and the other person, you are not doing it for the right person. If you are doing something that extends more of your energy than you can reasonably give, then you are giving too much. Make sure that you educate yourself on saying no and that you consciously clear your energy field from the request as well. This will protect you against the energy, the request, and the energy vampire. You also want to minimize the amount of time you spend around the energy vampire as much as possible and practice setting stronger boundaries with them in regards to what you are willing to listen to and engage with in order to create a stronger sense of protection against the energy vampire. This way, you do not feel like you are constantly in protection mode and you give yourself space to breathe and enjoy life.

Save Yourself from Time Vampires Too

In addition to energy vampires, there are also time vampires. Frequently, an energy vampire may also be a time vampire. However, not all time vampires are energy vampires. Time vampires are people who take up far too much of your time. You may find yourself constantly doing things for them, spending excessive time with them, or investing a great deal of time worrying about them. As a result, they end up taking up far too much of your precious time.

The best way to deal with a time vampire is to limit the time that you are willing to share with them. Decide what your boundary needs to be, set it, and stand behind it. Begin reinforcing it by only giving them the allotted amount of time and then saying no when the boundary is reached. This also counts when you are thinking about them. If you find yourself worrying about the person, say no to yourself and set a boundary with yourself as well. Reducing the amount of time you are willing to spend on a person, especially one that is toxic toward you (whether consciously or unconsciously) can support and protect you.

Even though it is nice to help people and you want to help others feel good in their lives, it is not your responsibility. Have an honest conversation with yourself about why you feel personally responsible for others and then begin to enforce boundaries with yourself as well. Creating these personal boundaries will make it easier for you to prevent yourself from feeling personally responsible for everyone else's needs and feelings. Then, it will become easier for you to say no and protect your time. When you do say no, make sure that you fulfill that time instead with something that is a genuine act of self-love. The more you take good care of yourself, the easier it is to understand why you deserve your time, energy, and attention even more than anyone else. Even if that does not feel natural or "right" to you in the beginning. Soon, you will understand that it is a necessary protection *and* self-care practice. Not only does it help you feel great, but it will also amplify your ability to help others.

Preserve and Protect Your Energy

It is important that you learn to preserve and protect your energy as an Empath. Knowing how to "tune out" of the world from time to time to give yourself the space to recharge is important. One great way to do this is through getting a high-quality set of noise-cancelling headphones and putting them on when you go out in public or when you are in noisy environment. While you may not be able to do this every time, using them in certain circumstances can support you in staying focused on the energy of the music rather than the environment around you. Consider using music that is uplifting and upbeat so that it actually amplifies your energy, rather than you going out and coming home feeling depleted.

Another way to protect your energy is to begin practicing energetic boundaries. This means that you make yourself unavailable to tune into the energies of those around you unless you give yourself permission to do so. Set the boundary with yourself that you are not going to tune into any energy.

Learning to switch your gift "on" and "off" can take practice, and the best way to do it is just to start. Soon, you will learn to be firm and consistent, and your boundaries will be effortless to uphold. This means that you begin gaining power and control over your Empath gift so that you no longer feel like you are being ruled by it. Instead, you can rule the gift and use it as you need to in order to support you in your life and soul purpose, as well as in leading a quality life.

Shield Your Aura

Shielding is a powerful practice that Empaths use to protect themselves from external energies. This is a form of creating an energetic boundary that can stay in place and keep you feeling protected without you always having to be consciously working toward it. In the beginning, your energetic shield may need continuous conscious reinforcement. Once you become more skilled with it, however, it becomes a lot easier.

The best shield to consider using when you are going out in public, or anywhere that your gift may be overly activated, is called a bubble shield. This shield is created by you envisioning a white light glowing in your solar plexus. This light then grows and grows, purifying your body and energy field and filling it with white light. Let this light grow until it forms a bubble that extends four feet away from your body in either direction, including down into the Earth. This shield is one that, once built, will stay in place as long as you desire. If you feel that your shield is down or you have taken it down by accident, you can always recreate it using the same strategy. Some people even choose to create a new one every morning to support them in staying protected throughout the day. Any time that you feel your energy is being threatened visualize your shield to reinforce it and keep unwanted energies out.

Leave Abusive Relationships

This can be challenging, but leaving abusive relationships is essential if you want to protect yourself as a human and as an Empath. If you are in an abusive relationship, whether it is with a family member, housemate, friend, spouse, or coworker, you need to take all measures possible to leave this relationship. These people are robbing you of your valuable energy and you need to do everything you can to protect yourself. Removing yourself completely from these people is the best solution. If you cannot leave the relationship for some reason, say you share custody of a child with your spouse or you cannot leave your job so you have to put up with your coworker, do everything you can to minimize contact to as little as possible. Then, give yourself the space, time, and resources to begin healing from the damage of this relationship.

If you are in a relationship with a narcissistic and abusive spouse, reading my book, "*"Emotional and Narcissistic Abuse: The Complete Survival Guide to Understanding Narcissism, Escaping the Narcissist in a Toxic Relationship Forever, and Your Road to Recovery"* will be extremely valuable to you. An important part of leaving relationships includes leaving them safely and seeking appropriate support in healing afterward. That book covers this in more depth.

Abusive relationships have the capacity to destroy an Empath from the inside out. They will destroy you mentally, physically, emotionally, and energetically. All of your gifts will be exploited, causing you to perceive them through jaded eyes. It can also damage your ability to use them as effectively, or as trustingly. Leaving these relationships will give you the space to heal and recover so that you can tap fully back into your gifts and use them to support you, uplift you, and assist you in achieving your goals throughout your life.

Carry Protective Crystals or Amulets
Something many Empaths do is carry protective crystals and amulets with them when they go out and about. Crystals come in many different varieties, each with unique purposes and abilities to support and protect your energies. Some of the most common ones for Empaths include:

- Amethyst: protects against anxiety and addictive behaviors.
- Obsidian: protects your aura against negative energy.
- Malachite: purifies your energy and promotes a cleaner and more free-flowing aura.
- Lepidolite: supports emotional healing and balance.
- Hematite: absorbs negative energy and calms stress in the body and mind.

Amulets are small ornaments or pieces of jewelry that are believed to protect against danger, evil, or disease. Some Empaths like to purchase these or create their own to wear with them when they go out in public. These support them in feeling confident and protected so that their energy bodies are not attacked or impacted during their daily activities. Depending on what they are made of, they can ward off unwanted energies, prevent you from stepping into and out of other people's energies unintentionally, and prevent you from feeling "blocked" in your energy field.

Chapter 10: Empathic Self-Care

"The deeper your self-love, the greater your protection."
- *Danielle Laporte*

Self-care as an Empath is essential. When you are an Empath, knowing how to rest, recharge, and cleanse your energies can promote a more fluid sense of well-being. These activities can release any energies you may be carrying, as well as produce a greater strength within you so that you can prevent unwanted energies from clinging to you in the first place. Stress and a poor self-care routine can easily result in individuals acquiring unwanted or harmful energies in the first place. So, reducing these and taking care of yourself can minimize the occurrence of this.

Here are some things that you need to begin doing to take care of your energies and keep yourself feeling nourished and supported.

Re-Charge Often
Recharging is an important way to keep your energies full. For an Empath, recharging often happens in nature or through direct rest. When you go into nature, connecting to the elements of the Earth around you can be highly supportive in allowing you to release any unwanted energies and refuel yourself with positive, beneficial energies. Many Empaths report feeling drawn to the forest often, regularly retreating to the forest to find peace and comfort. Some Empaths even recognize the word forest as meaning "for rest."

In addition to relaxing in nature and connecting with the elements, true rest through the form of sleeping can be deeply nourishing for an Empath. You can also spend time with your pets if you have any (which most Empaths do) as they seem to have a deep knowing over how they can support you in feeling nourished and whole. The unconditional love shared between you and your pets is truly nourishing when spending time together.

Many Empaths who are not actively caring for themselves well through recharging frequently will find themselves having disturbed sleep, either not sleeping enough or struggling to stay asleep all-night long. This comes from the chronic stress they are facing. By intentionally creating a stronger sleep routine and getting more sleep, Empaths can support themselves in feeling nourished and recharged so that they can go out and face the next day with confidence and ease.

Exercise Your Creativity

Despite Empaths being highly creative, some will actually shut down their creativity. This may occur from their childhood being abused or bullied around their creative talents, or it may happen occasionally if they are feeling overwhelmed and are struggling to dedicate enough time and attention toward creative outlets.

If you are someone who shuts down your creativity to avoid being bullied or hurt, it is a good idea to begin exploring and exercising your creativity once more. This process can help you awaken your energies again and begin expressing yourself in ways that you have been denying for a long time. Even just starting with something as easy as coloring is a great way to get started. Then, over time, you can move into your preferred mediums of creativity so that you can begin expressing yourself in the ways that feel best to you.

If you are in a funk and it has caused you to refrain from creating recently due to any number of excuses, recognize that the most likely reason is because you are struggling to actually express yourself. For Empaths, artwork is an essential form of self-expression. Naturally, if you stop creating it is important to look into the reason why. Then, you can begin to heal the block and practice creating again. Sometimes, it is as simple as setting aside some time, putting some music on and just doing it.

Consider Working for Yourself

Working for yourself as an Empath can be a powerful form of self-care. Being able to set your own hours and choose your own rules is empowering and can support you in having a positive work environment that enables you to create an income while feeling inspired and empowered to do so. Furthermore, if you feel a deep calling toward something in particular, such as healing or creating, you can create your own business doing just that. This means that not only do you free yourself from the restraints and toxicity of corporate jobs, but you also enable yourself to do what feels the best for you. This can have an even greater impact on your overall health than you may think, so be sure to consider it!

If you cannot leave your job or working for yourself does not seem reasonable at this time, consider going into business for yourself part-time. Even just creating artwork and selling it online or performing healing services here and there can be a great way to exercise your freedom, tap into your gift, and feel like you are gaining the benefits of working for yourself without losing some of the benefits that come with working for someone else.

Practice Energy Clearing Often
Energy clearing is an absolute must. When you are an Empath, energy clearing goes much beyond basic self-care. This is not just about feeling good, but about actually releasing energies that may be preventing you from doing so. Daily energy clearing practices, such as meditation or binaural beats, are extremely important. You should also have stronger antidotes on hand for those times when you feel that you are carrying an excess of energy and you need freedom from it. These "stronger dose medicines" of energy clearing are ones that may take longer, but will have a great impact on supporting your healing.

Meditate
Meditating is a powerful way of supporting yourself in clearing unwanted energies. Meditating for just ten minutes a day has been said to have a strong impact on supporting you in clearing all that you do not desire to carry with you, freeing your mind so that you can experience more peace and joy in the present moment.

If you find meditating to be challenging, you might consider using guided meditations or music to support you in your meditation practice.

Additionally, you may want to start with meditating for just a couple of minutes at a time, then gradually increasing the amount of time you are meditating until you reach ten minutes per day. This can make it easier for you to build this practice and support it in your daily life.

Hot Showers

Hot showers have a great ability to support you in releasing unwanted energies from your body. Using the hot water to cleanse and purify your body while envisioning all of the unwanted energies going down the drain can be very powerful in energy cleansing. Some people also use bath products that are infused with energy-cleansing materials, such as sage, himalayan salt, or various essential oils to support them in releasing energies. You can also find soaps that are infused with crystals that clear energies, too.

Himalayan Salt Baths

Himalayan salt is said to be great for drawing out toxins from the body, supporting you in releasing any energies that may be stored within your body and cells that are preventing you from clearing your energies effectively. If you do not have access to Himalayan salt, Epsom salts, dead sea salts, and Celtic sea salts are also excellent alternatives.

Binaural Beats

Binaural beats are a form of energetic music designed to support you in attuning yourself to certain energy frequencies. They can promote healing and balance, release energies, and support you in attuning you to virtually any frequency you desire. If you are clearing energies, using a binaural beat specific to clearing energies can be valuable. 536Hz and 432Hz are known to be good ones for energy clearing.

Get Energy Healing Done

If you are feeling particularly overloaded and like you need more support in releasing a great deal of energy, having an energy healing done by a healer can be powerful. Getting reiki or another energy clearing method done by a certified practitioner or Shaman can support you in releasing energies by bringing the skilled hand of a practitioner on board to help you. Think of it as a massage for your aura!

Clear Your Chakras

Chakras are energy meridians within the body that support various types of energies. We typically recognize seven energy chakras within the body: the root chakra by your tail bone, the sacral chakra by your navel, the solar plexus chakra just below your rib cage, your heart chakra in the center of your chest, your throat chakra in the upper part of your throat, your third eye chakra in the center of your forehead, and your crown chakra directly above the crown of your head. Each of these chakras represents a specific type of energy and needs to be balanced in order to maintain a positive energy flow.

Here is a basic cheat sheet to help you understand and balance the chakras:

- Root Chakra: associated with the color red. Grounding, eating deep red foods, walking on the grass bare footed and wearing the color red can support you in balancing this chakra.
- Sacral Chakra: associated with the color orange. Creativity, exercise, eating orange foods, and wearing the color orange can support you in balancing this chakra.
- Solar Plexus Chakra: associated with the color yellow. Building your confidence and self-esteem, reaching goals, eating yellow and citrusy foods, and wearing the color yellow can support you in balancing this chakra.
- Heart Chakra: associated with the color green. Opening your heart, healing your emotional body, and doing things that engage you in the energies of love and compassion, as well as eating green foods and wearing the color green can support you in balancing this chakra.
- Throat Chakra: associated with the color blue. Speaking your truth, confidence in saying what you mean, eating blue foods,

and wearing the color blue can support you in balancing this chakra.
- Third Eye Chakra: associated with the color indigo. Meditations that open your third eye, daydreaming, awakening your Empathic abilities, eating foods that are indigo and wearing the color indigo can support you in balancing this chakra.
- Crown Chakra: associated with the color violet. Praying, meditating, connecting to source, eating foods that are violet and wearing the color violet can support you in balancing this chakra.

In addition to these basic practices, you can also incorporate many other things such as essential oils, yoga, guided meditations, Reiki, and other practices in clearing and balancing these chakra energies.

Practice A Healthy Social Life

Engaging in a healthy social life and practicing positive activities is important for an Empath. Make sure that you are surrounding yourself with the right people who genuinely have your best interest at heart. You should also make sure that they are focused on assisting you in creating your best life possible.

Find and spend time with friends who will enjoy doing activities such as creating, attending positive social events, and engaging in activities such as yoga and meditation with you. While not all of your friends need to have these activities in common with you, having some that are willing to embrace your Empath path with you and join in on these activities can assist you in feeling supported and empowered by your friends.

Make sure that if you do have friends who are not entirely supportive that you minimize your time with them. You might have friends who are not entirely supportive, not because they are abusive but because they simply do not understand and relate. While you do not need to discard these friends, be mindful of how their beliefs and behavior impacts you and make sure that you refrain from spending too much time with them if they are having a negative impact on you. Do regular check ins to make sure that your friends are positive influences in your life and that you feel happy, supported, and empowered around them.

Thanks to the internet, you also have access to many online support forums and groups where you can connect with fellow Empaths around the world. This may even help you link up with local Empaths who understand you and can support each other. Take advantage of the resources available to you and be sure to find people who assist you in living your best life possible. Even if you naturally lean toward introverted tendencies, having a few people who you come out of your shell around and who you genuinely enjoy can be extremely beneficial to your overall wellbeing.

Take Advantage of To Do Lists

Any Empath who has not grown up educated on how to take care of themselves properly may find themselves feeling overwhelmed and even struggling to cope with feeling like a failure. This comes from having a lowered self-esteem and a sense of self-confidence. As such, setting and accomplishing goals can be extremely fulfilling for Empaths. This can also be a great way to bypass the mundaneness of routines and still get everything done.

Creating a to-do list each morning is a great way to provide yourself with a series of mini-goals that you desire to accomplish each day. Then, as you check things off the list, you will begin to feel fulfilled and satisfied. This can support you in having a deep sense of fulfillment, which is essential for Empaths. It can also support you in raising your self-esteem and self-confidence and in feeling more capable of achieving and accomplishing all that you desire to do.

In addition to creating daily to-do lists, it is wise to set weekly and monthly goals as well. These can provide you with larger goals that give you the opportunity to have even greater accomplishment in your life. The more you check off of these lists, the better you will feel.

Thus, you will begin to feel far more positive and better about yourself. This is both a great way to set aside all-day routines while still getting things done, and to feel great. For an Empath, this can even support you in breaking a mood swing or coming out of an energy funk so that you can begin to enjoy life once again.

Have a Gratitude Journal

Gratitude is a powerful energy that can support in recognizing and highlighting the parts of our lives that we love and enjoy. Keeping a gratitude journal can be a great way to support yourself in feeling better and caring for your energy. When you use a gratitude journal, you train your brain to focus on the positive *in addition to* the negative. It also allows you to reframe the negative. It is a great way to begin to see the silver lining and to develop a sense of optimism.

If you have never used a gratitude journal, you can start now by purchasing a journal and committing to writing in it daily or weekly, whatever suits you best. You can journal, brain dump, use bullet points, or otherwise write down what you are grateful for in any way that feels right for you. As long as you are consistent, you will find that it works great and supports you by promoting a more uplifted mood and a general sense of wellbeing. You should also write in your gratitude journal whenever you have a small win or celebratory moment in your life. Even giving thanks to the Universe is a great practice.

The other powerful thing about practicing gratitude is that it re-wires your brain to an appreciative and optimistic perspective. Over time by practicing this skill, you will notice you will have many more things to be grateful for.

Chapter 11: Ascending Earth Consciousness

"Your entire life has unfolded for your heart's ascension to love."
- *Bryant McGill*

We are living in the Aquarian Age: a time where Earth consciousness is being ascended. As a result, many more Empaths are incarnating into the world with the intention of assisting in shifting consciousness and supporting the awakening of others who are ready to ascend.

If you are an Empath who is presently awakening or who is already awakened to your gifts, there is a good chance that you are among the first to awaken with the intention of supporting others who are ready. This time can be a challenge for you since much of Earth is still inhabited by challenging, unkind, and even destructive individuals. It is important that you understand that your task is not to awaken everyone: it is to awaken those who are ready to be awakened. Remember, you awaken them by leading an awakened life, not by taking responsibility for their awakening and forcing it in any way.

At this time in society, we are beginning to recognize our own creative powers and natural talents. We are discovering that we are far beyond and above the very basic and destructive behaviors we have been portraying for many generations. We are ready to begin living a life in alignment with our energetic selves, realizing our fullest potential and living it out as we are here.

Some people who are awakening at this time are having great challenges with the energy. Of those awakening, you know there is so much better and yet it may cause deep aches within you in realizing that they are not. You may feel a lot of pressure to take on a significant amount of energy and "save the world." While that is what you are here to do, you are not here to do it alone. You do not have to take the weight of the entire world on your shoulders.

Because so many Empaths are incarnating at this time, there are large masses of Empaths prepared to work together toward the same goal: ascending Earth energies. This means that you can connect with other Empaths and work together with a group, rather than attempting to do it all yourself and exposing yourself to the massive amount of stress that this task would bring with it.

As an Empath, you may be noticing increasing energies lately. These energies are impacting all of Earth in the ascension of the collective and Earth itself. These symptoms may include things such as mysterious headaches, increased insomnia, fatigue, muscle aches, and other strange symptoms that are resulting from this. Some are also reporting feeling increased activity in their third eye, seeing visions and drawing on energetic information from the Universe. How you may be experiencing these symptoms ultimately depends on you. You may experience many, or none at all. This does not mean anything is wrong with you. Of course, any time you experience alarming symptoms with your physical or mental health you should always consult a healthcare professional. However, if it comes up that nothing is wrong, recognize that there is a good chance that it is just you experiencing the energetic ascension of Earth itself.

During the ascension process of Earth energies, it is important to take extra time nourishing your energies and taking care of yourself. As an Empath, you will be experiencing these energies more than anyone else. This means that you need to take extra precautions, while also ramping up your efforts to connect with yourself and lead by example. This is a great time to be awakening if you are presently in the process, even though you may be feeling many symptoms that make it feel otherwise. Know that these symptoms will not last forever. Your gift, however, will.

Final Words

Congratulations on completing *"Highly Sensitive Empaths: The Complete Survival Guide to Self-Discovery, Protection from Narcissists and Energy Vampires, and Developing the Empath Gift."*

Being an Empath is a great treasure that is only bestowed on those who can handle it. Since you were born an Empath, you can guarantee that this is a gift that you can manage well. Even if it has not felt that way yet, trust that it is only because there have not been enough resources available for you to support you in mastering this gift.

I hope this book becomes a great resource for you in supporting you in understanding yourself more. I also hope that you are now able to take advantage of better self-care tools to protect you and keep you feeling like you are giving from a full cup. If you have been dealing with abusive people in your life, I hope that you do take the time to understand that this is not because there is anything inherently wrong with you. Narcissistic people are drawn to you to as you have the one thing they do not: empathy. As a bonus, you've got a whole lot of it, too.

The next step for you is to take some time learning what self-care measures work best for you. While being an Empath is similar for everyone, you are still human and will still have different needs from others in your life. Creating a self-care method that supports your needs and allows you to feel truly nourished and cared for is important. Take your time working through different strategies until you find the routine that fits for you. Then, make sure that you always set aside time to fulfill that routine and keep yourself taken care of. It is essential that you always put yourself first, even though you may feel that this is "wrong" because of the way you are wired. Trust that if you want to help others, helping yourself first is the best way to do so. It is also important to realize that in many cases, the best way you can help is by becoming a role model. It is never helpful to anyone for you to take on the responsibility of others.

As well, be sure to take advantage of the many online communities that are built around being an Empath. With having access to the internet, taking advantage of these communities gives you the opportunity to meet and connect with other individuals who have similar experiences as you. This will ensure that you are able to access support and understanding from other Empaths. As an Empath, not having other Empaths in your life who speak the same language as you can be challenging. It may even lead you to feeling isolated. Having access to those who will understand and show the same degree of Empathy and compassion that you do when you are experiencing things in your life can be extremely helpful.

Being an Empath can be challenging if you do not have access to the right resources, but once you do, you begin to see the blessing and beauty in the gift that you have been given. Be sure to give yourself the opportunity to fully flourish in your gift so you can live your best life.

Lastly, if you enjoyed the book *"Highly Sensitive Empaths: The Complete Survival Guide to Self-Discovery, Protection from Narcissists and Energy Vampires, and Developing the Empath Gift"* please take the time to leave a kind review on Amazon. Your honest feedback would be greatly appreciated.

Thank you, and best of luck in your journey.

If you forgot to sign up to the newsletter and receive you free eBook on "6 Ways to Thrive as an Empath and Live a great Life" here is the link below.

http://bit.ly/6WaysToThriveAsAnEmpath

CPSIA information can be obtained
at www.ICGtesting.com
Printed in the USA
LVHW081156040819
626449LV00021B/3007/P

9 781794 429482